Sidewalk Saints

life portraits of the

New Orleans Street Performer Family

Jim Flynn

Curbside Press

The Straight up Word
From the Lowdown Curb

sidewalksaints.com

to
my loving family

with
special thanks to

David Weinberg
Katya Apekina
Danny Laurino
Peter Spring
Marzipan
Derek Bridges
Stanley Garczynski
Nelson Hall
Harriette Prevatte
Jack Ox
New Era Brass Band
Bob Arihood
Eli Pritykin

I apologize to all of the wonderful performers who do not appear in this first edition. This is not a reflection on the validity of your stories but on the constraints of space and time.

watch videos and post messages
for these performers at

sidewalksaints.com

Table of Contents

Break Dancing

Statues, Cowboys and Characters

Puppets

Tarot and Palm Readers

Instant Photography

Sidewalk Astronomy

Just Pictures

Keith "Wolf" Anderson from New Orleans

Most every younger musician in this city, I've taught them. The good ones, the bad ones, everybody, I've taught them. It's like Louis Armstrong said about seeing babies cry and you watch them grow. You watch the youngsters learn, and then pretty soon you learn from them. I've seen that happen with a lot of these youngsters. Now I'm asking them, how do you do this? How do you do that?

My family was from here, but they had moved up to Chicago before I was born. When I was nine, we came down here for Mardi Gras season. I saw all the little kids out on the streets playing their horns. Man, I never saw anything like that in Chicago. All I saw up there was gangs and people shooting dice on the corner. This was another world. I didn't wanna leave, so I ended up staying down here in the Treme with my grandma. My mamma bought me a coronet before she left. I'll always thank my mother for that, because that's what made me the man I am today.

They started me off in the jazz program at Bell Junior High. Six month later, not only was I in the concert band, I was in the marching band too. I'm a fast learner. In school I was a bookworm. I said, let me hang around with the geeks, the guys that have some brains. The tough guys, they can have that life. I'm telling you the truth. I didn't drink my first beer till I was twenty-three years old.

School gave me the foundation, but as far as really learning how to play, that came from cats in the neighborhood. In the Treme music was like oxygen in the air. I was like a sponge, I couldn't help but absorb it. Late at night I used to pretend like I was going to sleep and then sneak outta the house to hear different cats play. I caught a lot of whippings. My ass was sore, but looking back I see that it was worth it.

I had a lot of mentors, but my number one mentor was Anthony Lacen, better known as Tuba Fats. He was like an encyclopedia of New Orleans music. He could play it all from the 1890's to the new stuff. He was hard core. If Tuba wanted you to learn a part, you better learn that part. If you had a gig with Tuba, you better show up with your black and whites and a suit and a tie. If you showed up wrinkled, he'd

Keith "Wolf" Anderson

send you home.

I played with all sorts of cats. When I played with the older guys, sometimes they'd take some woman's eyeliner and give me a little peach fuzz mustache so that I could go in and play the clubs.

The first time I played with the cats from Rebirth was back in high school. At the time they were calling themselves The Group. I had me a little job working at this seafood plant down by the projects. Man, I used to be stinking from messing with fish all day. One night, I was walking home and I heard brass band music coming from outta this house. I walked in and it was Philip Frazier, Keith Frazier and Kermit Ruffins. I said, "Y'all sound good. You should play some jazz, make yourself some money." At first they were all cheesing on me because I was stinking like dead fish, but then I picked up that horn and they saw that I could play. They started calling me Wolf, saying I looked like a wolfman with my sideburns and shit. At first I didn't like it, but now I'm used to it.

I've always been a sideman. I've never been a leader. I don't like to get involved in the politics of the band. I'm still like that today. Right now, I'm with the Dirty Dozen, but if we don't have no gig, I'll play with anybody. If you wanna play, I'm gonna play.

When I was coming up, I never had a problem playing with white musicians. My family always told me that it wasn't about black or white, it was about wrong or right. Not everybody had that attitude. Sometimes, I'd show up for gigs and they'd say, look y'all can play, but he can't. I didn't have the complexion for the connection. The racism has always been a frustration to me, but I just channel it through my music. I just play it out. I play some stuff sometimes and it makes me cry. And I'm a man and I'm macho, but when I play music and I know it's from the heart, it makes me cry.

Over the years I've played with every top brass band in the city. After Rebirth I went to Dirty Dozen, then Olympia, then to The Hot Eight and now I'm back with Dirty Dozen. I've been all over the world and met all kinds of people. Europe, Asia, I even been to Papua New Guinea. Over there, they said that we had to stay in the taxi, because they still had headhunters running around who might roast us on a spit. I'm telling you, I've seen a lot of crazy things and a lot of beautiful things. I've played with a lot of beautiful people.

Sidewalk Saints

I don't care how far my music takes me, if I don't have a gig, you'll always find me out here playing on these streets. There's no captive audience on the streets. It's like a den of lions and you gotta go in there and fight. On the streets you can't fake the game on credit. Average tourist don't know that I been all around the world and played for thousands of people. They don't know who I am, but they know that I'm playing from the heart. To me, that's all that matters.

Keith Wolf Anderson

Aaron Paulin from New Orleans

Ain't no frowning when I'm playing this here. When it's time to play, it's time to play. I'm telling you, there ain't nothing greater. Boom! Boom! Boom! I'm the purveyor of the thunder! Couple years ago, I got hit by a firecracker right before the Sugar Bowl Parade. I had to wear the strap right across the burn. It hurt something terrible, but as long as the band was playing, I didn't feel a thing.

My daddy was Doc Paulin. He been leading brass bands in New Orleans since the 1920's. Out of my ten brothers, six of us played in my daddy's band, all different instruments. Pops, he played trumpet. He was the leader of the band and everything, but I was always standing right there by the drum section. I remember my momma used to cook Sunday dinner, and we'd be sitting there at the dinner table, and then all the sudden I hear something outta my ear two three blocks away. I'm like, that's my daddy. I'm gonna go watch my daddy. Now, if Pops seen me he's gonna run me off. You don't miss my momma's Sunday dinner. Uh Uh. No. You there. So what I used to do is hide right there behind my cousin Tommy banging on that bass drum.

First time I played in a parade? Oh Lord. Here we go. I just made my sixteenth birthday. It was the night before Mardi Gras and I hear the phone ring at four o'clock in the morning. Now you know when you get a call at four o'clock in the morning, you're thinking the worst. It was my daddy's snare drummer. He said Doc, I can't make it, had too much to drink. For Pops that was the worst. He stomping up and down, hot blessed, Lord what I'm gonna do? All the sudden he came in the room. Ripped the covers off me. He says, you coming with me today. I said, Lord have mercy! I started sweating. My momma got up, she broke out the ironing board and was ironing the black and whites. I'm in there shaking like a leaf on a tree. Like a leaf! I said, Pop are you sure? He told me, shut up! You're coming with me today. Shut up! I shut up. That was the thing to do, or either get a good right cross from Pops. I kinda knew deep down that's what I wanted to do — but not on MARDI GRAS DAY! In front of millions!

We got to the Corner Club at Second and Annunciation about six o'clock in the morning. We was supposed to be on the street

photo: Derek Bridges

for seven o'clock. The rest of the guys started showing up and they said look, we gonna have another snare drum player, you just follow behind him till you get to know what's happening. The other snare drum player, he chomping on a cigar. "Eh boy, don't worry bout nothing, but don't mess up, ya hear?"

It had to be thirty degrees outside. It was cold and I'm sweating buckshot. I'm looking at the clock. Six forty, six forty-five, six fifty. My heart is pounding, boom, boom, like a drum. My hands are clammy. Here we go! Going down the road, I'm chip chip chipping, trying not to mess nobody up.

Now the other snare drummer, he had a old lamb skin head, and in the cold weather you loosen it up so it won't split on you. He didn't do that. It was about eight thirty, nine o'clock that morning, WHOP! His head split half in two. Right down the middle. I said, Lord you got me on this one. You got me. Pops turned around, looked up at me from his trumpet. I told him, lets go. I'll never forget that. That was, oh boy, I'll tell you. From that day, that was it. I knew this is what I wanted to do for the rest of my life. That's been thirty-five years ago. Haven't stopped since.

After me came my brother Ricky, he started playing snare right alongside me. I remember we was playing at the Jolly Bunch Parade and Ricky busted open his head and he turned it over and went to beatin on the side. All the hardware came off, left a trail. Beat that thing to death. Brother wasn't gonna say die. He's like me, take after Pops. Just because it ain't working that don't mean it's not playable. After Ricky come Dwayne. Oh, I tell you what, that boy know he can play some trombone. Tat! Ohwee! Next one was Scott, that's another trombone player. You talk about some licks? Ohhh, sweet, sweet, sweet, Pow! Next one was Phillip — trumpet. Pop was waiting on that one, somebody gotta play trumpet in here, and you the one. I tell you what, you couldn't ask for better. Next one up, Rodrick. Now I might be prejudice, because that's my brother, but that's the baddest saxophone I ever heard.

When I was coming up, the brass bands in New Orleans was going through a transition. Instead of everybody dressing up in black pants, white shirts and hats, you had bands that didn't have no uniform. My daddy called that the rainbow division. That's not the way it ought to be. No. Instead of playing the traditional songs, they were playing more pop songs. I was younger and didn't know no better, so I wanted to play what everybody else was playing. Pops was like, we gonna stick with the tried and true. Keep doing what you're doing.

Now I see where Pops was coming from, because it's getting hard to find a good traditional New Orleans brass band. These days you're not gonna find a jazz funeral the way it's supposed to be done. That's a very solemn thing. You don't go out there second lining even before everything started, taking the casket throwing it up and down. That's not the way we were taught. No. You very seldom see it. It's like, damn, where's it going?

That tradition has to be held down. If we let that slip away, then that's taking away from everybody that went before us. What kind of testament would that be if we're not doing it the way they did it in their time? I'm traditional to the end.

I guess I'd have to say the high point in my musical career was in 2006. We'd been through hell with Katrina, but somehow we managed to get The Paulin Brothers' Brass Band back together to do a gig at Preservation Hall. Pops was ninety-nine years old, so he wasn't playing with the band, but he was sitting up on stage with his cane. In the middle of "Bye Bye Blackbird," Pops just stood up right on stage. That did it. That gave me the recognition. Oh man, I tell you, I get goose bumps just thinking about it.

Pops passed November past, one hundred years old, and he still had good right cross. I felt the breeze from that a few times, I tell you.

Right now it's kinda hard to find a good solid gigs with a brass band. Lately, I been coming down to Jackson Square and playing for tips. Pops never really approved of that there, because you can't get the real sound with just two or three musicians. Don't go halfway, do it right. That was his outlook on it. If I could be out here with a ten-piece band, I would, but I gotta do what I gotta do.

Hear those bells in the cathedral? The wedding must just be getting out. I'm gonna run over there and see if that band needs a bass drummer.

Hey! Whose leg I gotta break to get a gig with y'all?

Mark "Tuba" Smith from New Orleans

A lotta people is scared of the tuba. They say it's too big, it's too heavy, let me play a trumpet, let me play a saxophone. But me, I see that tuba as a challenge. See with the tuba you have to fight with that tuba and that tuba gonna make you a man. I'm telling you, in my forty years playing tuba, I've had all kinda ups and downs and in betweens, but one thing I ain't never did was put this tuba down.

During Katrina, I had lost me the neck to my old tuba, and I was up in Texas using a piece of garden hose to stick the mouthpiece. The thing is all bouncing up and down. I had to stick my hand up to hold the hose and my hand got stuck like that. I can't move my left hand — but I ain't let it stop me from playing. Oh no. I'm sitting down eating dinner, everybody say, Tuba what's wrong with your hand? I said, man, just leave me alone, I can't move the shit.

I get back to New Orleans, they had agencies was giving away instruments to all the musicians. Everybody getting brand new horns, but me and a brand new horn. Oh no. A new horn you gotta nurse it like a baby. The horn gotta grow up with you. I ain't got time for that shit. I said let me get this here tuba, some forty years old, donated from Wichita, Kansas. Everybody saying, Tuba what's wrong with you getting that old horn? Let me tell you something, ain't nothing like a horn that's ass done been whipped and beat up on. That way before the horn can beat me up, I'm beating up on the horn. It's gotta have the seasoning, the flavor. Just like frying chicken. You can't fry no chicken unless that skillet been seasoned. See, with chicken they got something called Tuba's chicken, you know my momma and daddy done taught me. And that's the best damn chicken. Now, I could tell you how to make Tuba's chicken, but you go home and your chicken ain't gonna taste the same. Why? Cause you ain't go the same pot. Your pot ain't been seasoned. See, me and my music done been seasoned. I gotta have me a horn that got the same flavor.

I was born and raised in the Magnolia Projects, nineteen hundred and fifty nine. They closed Magnolia down because all the violence, but back then it wasn't like that. People had a winning attitude. If a young man wanted to do something with his life, then

Mark "Tuba" Smith

11

the people was gonna help him. I was brought up right. Whatever I wanted to do, my people was gonna be there for me. You know what I wanted to do? Play tuba.

Picked up my first tuba in the old hurricane shelter at Thomy Lafon Middle School right across the street. It was in the back corner all dusty ain't been played in years. I put that big old tuba to my mouth and WHOOMP! First time I tried. Man, I just loved that sound. Used to practice my tuba walking from project to project WHOMP! WHOMP! WHOOMP! I went all the way from Magnolia down to the Seventh Ward. I got so good that everybody wanted me in they band. I had a name that just wouldn't quit. Something about me, I was like the golden child, like I had a beam of light coming down on that tuba.

My momma was my motivator. I'm the baby. Wasn't nobody messing with me. She had a little twenty-two on her side, you mess with my baby, momma shoot you and all that crazy stuff. When they hired me for a gig, they had to go through Ernestine Smith to get to me. Let me tell you, my first bar room gig, I'm no more than seventeen years old, my momma came running out to the car saying, "Don't you never come and get my baby out there playing at this hour." Ain't nobody didn't mess with my momma.

Tuba gives some pointers to the Young New Orleans Traditional Brass Band

My first band was Doc Paulin. He taught me all the traditional. Man, I had that down solid. Then here come the Dirty Dozen, playing that funk. I said, man, I wanna play me some of that there. Now Doc Paulin, he said no no no, that ain't no good. I said I gotta do my own thing, so I went and joined The Pinstripe Band. Man, we were the baddest thing on the street. I used to dance with the tuba getting down on my knees, shaking and crawling doing all that acrobatic shit. Man, we was funky!

You play in a traditional band, they want you to play way down low. Bluuurp Bluuurb Bluuurp Bluuurb. You just holding it down and the other horns got the melody. I'm playing with the Pinstripe, I say that I'm still gonna hold me down that Bluuurp Bluuurb, but let me get some of that Ba Dippy Doo Bop. I'm playing all over that chord. See, I was playing how I feel. Never played it the same way twice, 'cause I never felt the same way twice. Everybody else in Pinstripe is doing they own thing too. Man, that band wasn't nothing nice. Uptown, downtown people were amazed. We got big, playing on television, we went on tour in Europe. We were at a gig in Spain and I stepped on a old rusty nail backstage. My foot got all infected, and they had to send me back home.

Now I ain't gonna lie. Sometimes when the music gets slow, you have to have something else to fall back on. Growing up, I used to sell cold drinks or cut grass. They used to have a program in the projects where kids could get a lawn mower. But now, I'm a grown man. I said, I think I'm gonna follow in my daddy's footsteps, be a working man. I'm gonna go to Southern University, be a chef.

I went to college and met my wife. She played basketball for Louisiana Tech. I always did like strong women. I was in one of these little frat things, and they set my ass up. They said, Tuba, "This broad so fine, I bet you ain't never gonna fool with her."

Know what I told 'em? "Boy I can win her over." And I did, I went into her real sweet and she was kinda throwed off, because she wasn't used to that. We got married. Had a daughter.

We're raising our daughter. I got me a job working as a chef at the Maison Dupuy. But my wife, she started to develop a attitude. See, when she was growing up her daddy was a long shore man, and she watched her daddy beat up her mama and her mama jumped off a bridge when she was like twelve, thirteen-years-old. She's like, I ain't never letting no man do me like that. She stared developing a attitude where she gonna beat up her man. Every man she was with, cut his tires, beat him up. She started beating on me, I got a divorce. I'm all over it, but we got a child together. Jesus Christ, that's a rough road.

After that, I said I'm gonna get back into playing more tuba. Started going down to Jackson Square. That's where you had the man with the plan, Tuba Fats. He used to have twelve, thirteen people down there. Tuba Fats, he had a big heart. He did not discriminate. But if you're gonna play with Tuba Fats, you gotta play the way he want you to. But see, me, I can't play the tuba like nobody else. I'm gonna play the song, but it gonna sound different. I'm gonna do me. They say, that don't sound like the same song we playing. I said, yes it is, but they still screaming and hollering, trying to send my ass home. You get tired of getting your ass whipped. So you know what I said? I had the nerve and the guts to tell Tuba Fats and the rest of the band, you all suck out my face. I'm staying. I'm gonna play. I'm gonna show you. So, Tuba Fats, he tell me to go ahead and play. He made everybody be quiet, gave me the opportunity to play all by myself. I played from my heart and they respected that. They said man, you're crazy but you can stay. After that they started calling me The Missing Link, saying I look like a cave man and shit.

In '91 my momma died. Then in '92 my daddy died. Man that hit me hard. For a while I couldn't do nothing but sit there. That was the hardest thing I ever been through. Man, I tell you that was rough times. I'm not even gonna get into all the shit I been through and I put myself though. But you know what helped me? Getting on that bus and coming down to Jackson Square. That's where the people know me. I'm telling you, these people out here on these benches are like my family.

Mark "Tuba" Smith

Photo: Irwin Thompson courtesy of The Dallas Morning News

9/2/05 Tuba heads for the bus to Texas after being rescued by boat and taken to the Convention Center.

Glen David Andrews from New Orleans

Man, it's good to be back in the Treme. Since Katrina, I been living all over the place, but nothing beats being back home. You heard me playing down in the Quarter, but I brought you out here to see where the music come from. You gonna see the real shit. We gonna walk over to Tuba Fats Square.

That there is Craig Elementary, that's where I went. Oh, hey, that's my second grade teacher, I'm her best student. Hey Miss Metoe! That's right, I'm doing good for myself. You taught me right. That over there that's Fish Lastie, he play the drums down at Preservation Hall. We supposed to get together and play over at his house tomorrow. Miss K-Doe! That's Ernie K-Doe's wife, Antoinette K-Doe. She the coolest. She say she gonna get some flowers for the square. I'm telling you everybody know everybody in the Treme Neighborhood.

So this is Tuba Fats Square. Before Tuba Fats die, he made this piece of land a real park, a place for folks to come out the house, shed on the lot and have a good time. Ten years ago, if you came down to this corner you'd a seen a crowd of musicians all day everyday. Between here and St. Bernard there used to be twenty bars and all of them had live music. Most of them is closed now. We fighting to bring it back, but they got people who wanna re-gentrify the neighborhood and kill the music. Last year, I got arrested for singing at Kerwin James' funeral right here in Tuba Fats Square.

I was born right round the corner. My momma was standing on the porch, and she started dancing to a second line parade and her water bag broke. My family's still all around here. My father, he 'round the corner right now. He's a gambler, ordinary dude, didn't stay with my mamma. You know how that story leads up for most young black men, so this is the same story. A lot of my uncles is my influence, because they played music. My momma? She cool as hell. I'm waiting on her to come get me in a few. Typical mother, be worried about me. You know, in the streets, don't get in no trouble.

When you're a kid in the Treme, you do like you see. You get up every Sunday and everybody be leaving out the door to go to church or a second line, probably both. I can't never remember not

wanting to be a musician. That's all I wanted to do and that's all I been doing. I don't think I just do it good. Actually, I think I do it great.

I done played with more bands than I can remember. I done played Preservation Hall. Not only did I do it, but I did it with my own band. I do it all, blues, jazz, funk. I just did my own gospel album at Zion Hill Baptist Church right 'round the corner.

I ain't lying, I wanna be traveling regular, a tour bus, everything. I think it's my time, but there's a lot of personal issues I'm dealing with. One thing I know, is no matter what, you're always gonna hear Glen Andrews in the Treme, 'cause you gotta come out here and blow fire. You got top grade musicians from all over the world come here and they can't catch this groove for nothing. Then you gonna see a little boy and he gonna jump up and be knocking fire at your ass.

I'm telling you, I don't love nothing like I love the Treme. Ask anybody out here, they gonna tell you ain't never gonna find another neighborhood like this. I'm gonna tell you you ain't never gonna find another musician like me.

Joseph Maize Jr. from New Orleans

I'm straight out the projects, St. Bernard, Seventh Ward. Eighteen years in there before Katrina. In the projects it's just get it how you live. However you living, that's how you getting it. You killing? Watch your back from getting killed, you heard? If you selling drugs? Watch your back from the jackers, you heard? But you know if you playing music, everybody inspired by you. Mostly everybody in the hood, they like come tell me, man I wish I'd a stayed stuck with that horn bro, this ain't the life, don't do what I'm doing.

Coming up, my family was always straight cause my momma liked to work. She wasn't never taught to go to school to get a job, but she would just get out the house and work. My father, he was smoking crack for a while. I feel like sometimes he let us down, but now he keeps us up too. He's still with us, everything lovely right now. I'm telling you, my family's better than anybody's family. Anybody. You heard?

This band is like a family too, been together since ninth grade at George Washington Carver. Our band director, Mr. Wilbur Rawlins, he actually came to my house before school started. I get home from band camp one day, Mr. Rawlins is sitting in my living room, got my momma all bucked up on me playing in the band at Carver. Mr. Rawlins can talk. He got a mouthpiece on him. You heard?

Mr. Rawlins run that band like the army. Be all you can be. After you done blown all the songs, and you ain't got nothing left, he turn the air conditioning off and make you blow 'em one more time. You be wanting to quit, but then you're coming down Canal Street at the end of that parade, and everybody gonna know that band gonna blow. I'm telling you, Mr. Rawlins was almost like a father figure, just feeding off the stuff he do and how he carries himself make you wanna be a better person.

Springtime of 2002, the band was going on a trip. We all excited to go, but it cost seventy dollars. Not all of us had that kinda cash, so we all got together and went out to the Jazz Fest and started playing the streets. We only had three shabby old horns and everybody else was banging on cardboard boxes. In two or three hours, we had

the money for the trip. We were like damn, let's go out on Bourbon and make some money for ourselves. We set right up on Bourbon and Canal, and I ain't lying, we just blew them tourists' minds. That money just started rolling into that box. Now I got friends working at McDonald's, whatever, making minimum wage, but I'm getting paid for my music. I love this here, you heard? We started hitting it everyday. Since I was sixteen, everything I need come from out that tip box. I even bought me a car. I'm telling you, if you were a member of To Be Continued Brass Band, your mamma really didn't have to do nothing for you. I was helping her out with the bills here and there.

To Be Continued Brass Band got it's name from Big Al Carson. One day we was marching down Bourbon Street having our own little parade and Big Al called us all into the Funky Pirate and he asked us play "The Saints." Going out the door, Big Al was like, "What's y'all's name?" We told him we ain't really have a name yet, so he yelled out, "To Be Continued!"

Yeah. We likeded that, To Be Continued, because no matter what, this band is gonna keep going. The core of our band is too strong, you can't stop it. You heard?

When we heard about Katrina, my family knew we wasn't

gonna evacuate. We ain't got no money, we ain't got nowhere to go. We all laid out up on the third floor and that project is solid brick. It's like the Hulk you heard? Our first floor neighbors, we invited 'em in to stay with us. Everybody in the neighborhood who lived in houses was running into the projects and somebody would take 'em in.

When the storm hit, we just rolled it out. That wind is howling, but none of our windows ain't blow out. Them projects is Ford tough. Every single brick project made it through the storm. The first floor got flooded out, but that ain't nothing. They could fix that. I don't know why the city closed down St. Bernard after the storm. They fake.

After Katrina, everybody in the band is all over the country, Texas, Virginia, California. I'm down in Houma, I lost my trombone, so I ain't played for four months. I'm going to school out there and I got me a little job working as a janitor. Everybody in the band is going through they own trial and tribulations. A lot of us ain't never really been out of New Orleans before. There's a lot of opportunity, but it ain't home. So we're like, we gotta go do us, we gotta come back and get this together.

When we get back to New Orleans, we staying in hotel rooms, all ten in one room. You know if they be lettin' ten people in one room, you is staying where the crack heads at. Wherever you fall asleep, on the bed or the floor, that's where you at. For six months, that's how we did, 'til everybody get on they feet. That'll take a wear and tear on your body. People look at us and say, damn, how do y'all keep a ten piece band together? It's cause we done been through all that shit. Now we know once all us ten in together, in any city, ain't nothing gonna stop us from doing us.

When we first got back on Bourbon, it was dry. Dry. The vibe wasn't right. Instead of tourists, it was a lot of Mexicans. Police treating us different. MPs everywhere with big guns. Nobody's not tipping, but we alright 'cause we ain't doing it for the money, we just doing it for us. Bit by bit, the city started turning back to regular. Ask me, right now I'd say it's back.

In the last two years we played at Jazz Fest. We even did a tour in Spain. I ain't like the plane ride, but, man, those people were tipping heavenly. We was blowing everybody's minds. Balboa, the whole town came out to hear us. I'm like damn, we the same band that was beating

on boxes out on the street three years ago.

I think what make this band different than any other brass band in the city is the era we came up in. Everybody gangster, whowling out. Hard was what was in. It's like Soldier Slim said, "If you was off the porch in '94," meaning you was doing your thing, killing whatever, "and in '95 you made it out. Then you're a real nigga." Growing up, that's all we looking at.

We still living in the hood, and we still trying to get it, but since we come up through all that crazy shit, we gonna be extra positive coming out of it. You look at us, everything is just too authentic, just raw and real swagging. Like just straight up, if you just sit there and hear us play, and groove with that second line funk, you gonna blow your goop, you heard?

Brandon "B" Franklin from New Orleans

My daddy played the saxophone back in high school. I ain't never heard him play, cause he don't fool with it no more. He had too many kids, so he had to work to take care of us. I felt him, so I said I'm gonna play saxophone. Got my first horn in seventh grade at Colton Middle School. Miss McGowen and Mr. Haynes, man they could teach. By eighth grade I was drum major, leading the whole band. I got to Carver and the band, we ran that school. We could be on the yard making trouble and ain't nobody mess with us, because come parade season we the ones y'all gonna be following representing for Carver.

First time I played on Bourbon, I was spooking. From number one, I know my daddy, he don't want me to be out here. And then it's just wild out here, it's bust open. I missed a lot of the early part on the strain of my daddy not wanting me to be out there, but now that's all I be doing. Music all day so you know that's how I gotta get it. Ya feel me? Straight off the dump. I ain't about to get up everyday and jump on the back of trash truck to make a dollar to survive.

My people don't really want me to do it. They want me to go to school, get the education and all that. After Katrina, I went back and

University Hospital medical resident Andrew Abrass sits in with TBC.

got my high school diploma, but college, I'm putting that aside. I just wanna pursue this right quick, cause it just might be that break.

Right now my baby momma, we split up on the strain of my music. She ain't like the fact that I'm always gone, this, that and the other. I go out of town, she think I'm hitting something, you heard? But it ain't about that, it's not to get no stripes, it's just that I got to do what I gotta to do. I know I gotta support my son, and I know music is gonna be it, so I gotta get with it.

My son, man, this dude gonna be something special. He's liable to be the president. I'm serious, he got that glow. Love that dude, man. I ain't seen him in a week though. His momma been playing games with me, trying to keep him from me. I'm trying to humble myself on that situation, 'cause I know whatever goes down with me and his momma, I'm gonna be there for that dude.

I'm gonna be straight up with you, when TBC first started playing, we ain't really practice, we just out there joking around and playing straight from the gut. For a lot of these guys, that's still all they want to do. But me, I'm twenty-one, and I know what's up with life. I know if we're gonna make it as a band, we gotta be moving in new directions.

Sidewalk Saints

Me personally, I wanna take this here music to Mars. I'm getting deep into classical music, bebop, that elevator music, like Kenny G. Don't talk about that, that's gonna do, I love that. People in the band be joking on me, but I don't give a fuck. Say what you want about B. I'm gonna do me. Anybody that can teach me something, I'm gonna listen. Like, if we out there on Bourbon and somebody wanna step in with the band, I don't have a problem with that, cause I might snatch something from you. If you can play, I'm gonna try and learn something from you.

Music bro, to me it's the best thing that God ever created. I put that horn in my mouth and I'm jolly. Coming home from practice, I'm jolly. Just listening on my iPod, I'm jolly. This all I got, so you know I gotta get it. You heard me? They gonna know about TBC and Brandon Franklin. Ya feel me? It's coming up.

Straight off the dump.

Edward "Juicy" Jackson III from New Orleans

I'm from New Orleans and I'm out the hood. Ninth Ward, Desire and Galvez. I'm out the hood, but I ain't out the slum slum, you know what I'm saying? But just put it like this, the stuff that's normal to me ain't normal to you. My mamma kept me away from all that little crazy stuff to the best of her ability, but we was living in a double shotgun. RIGHT NEXT DOOR you got all the vics in the hood smoking that pipe, that beam me up Scottie. Me being eleven, twelve-years-old, I'm seeing grown ass men geeked up shivering on the floor. I'm telling you, I done seen people smoke that pipe, shoot that dope, and that's why I didn't never did it.

My daddy, man. My daddy. Boy, my daddy did everything I don't need to be doing. Let's just put it like that. I ain't got to go do it, he done it. That boy went served his jail time. Got out and we was straight for six months. We was building up and doing our thing and they got me. We was straight. Then mommy and daddy got into it. Watched him whoop her ass. Got it all rolled out, you know what I'm saying? That boy went to jail. They convicted him, cause he din done too much. You just gotta go sit now. You gonna sit the rest of your probation. So he went sit there five flat, all three hundred and sixty five of 'em. Every time.

Once you come out, I'm in high school. There ain't nothing you can really tell me, cause you din miss that point, that make or break point. You done missed all that. Now, I'm really at the point to where this is the time where you were supposed to let me be. You know what I'm saying, but good thing you know the Lord had me in the band. I had people around me that was good mentors and good teachers and stuff like that. I wasn't around that just throwed off person influencing me as a young black man.

Me personally, I ain't never hang with nobody in my age bracket, cause they stupid. Somebody's older and wiser, that's people I like to be around. Like Mister Jerry McGowen, he taught me at McDonogh15, great drummer. He went to Carver, so he instilled that Carver in me. So from that point on I went to Carver. That's where I knew I was going, so straight out of elementary, I hit the high school scene.

I come down to Bourbon, these guys is out there playing. They all already in Carver. I'm in seventh grade. I'm not supposed to be nowhere around, but I done learned the snare drum, I can play the tuba, all the brass horns. What I used to do, I used to take every cold song that was going down out here, and I used to write 'em, every part of the sheet music. I can go in and play any position, I'm like Reggie Bush. When they had a spot open on trombone, I was like the first round draft pick.

I get to Carver everybody was in cahoots, we was cooling. We ain't have all the stuff the other schools had, but it was a good school in terms of raising a real black man that you need out here today. They was on your back, but they wasn't trying to harm you. They understood where you was coming from when you was at home, they understood when you out it that day. And like me, I'm a smart guy, I'm walking around with like a three point five. I'm in the Carver Band, and I'm telling you everybody know already we the best band in the city. It was getting to the point where we was calling ourselves Carver University. When you go back and think about it, the storm it probably had to hit. 'Cause like the level we was about to take New Orleans band to was just gonna make band everywhere else uncivilized.

Only reason I graduated high school was 'cause of TBC. After the storm all our transcripts is messed up 'cause the school got closed. I'm doing my junior year out in Dallas and they was trying to make me take classes that I done already passed. Same thing happened to everybody in the band, and for a lot of us that's the reason we ain't all got diplomas. One night, I'm out here playing on Bourbon, and I seen my teacher. He got it straightened out for me.

My senior year, I come back to New Orleans, my momma's still back in Texas. I'm living with the band and going to McDonogh 35. Miles College in Alabama was offering me this money to be in the music program. Now coming up, I never did wanna learn none of that honkey donk. That's how I put it. We just out there playing and we ain't trying to calculate. We just trying to knock — pure and natural love music. You can't pick up a book and get that. You gotta go to second lines. You gotta play the street. You gotta hang with Wolf, you heard? So I got all this understanding, but I can't explain how I know what I know. It was like I had a dictionary with just definitions, no words. So

I figure I'm gonna go to Miles and find out what that's all about. Went there for two semesters, got that structure. I could have kept going, but why not take that knowledge back to TBC? I don't wanna really play with no other band.

Since I been back, people been calling me maestro, 'cause I got all this technical knowledge. But don't get it twisted, TBC don't have no leader. Every decision we make, all ten gotta agree. If one person don't agree, we gotta find out what he's talking about and that's how we learn so much from each other. It be like one body talking with one voice.

If you look at all the shit we done been through in the last three years, I'm thinking God must have had it in his plans to keep TBC rolling. Every time before we play we all come together and we pray. Every time. We know we blessed. I'm telling you, this ain't just a band.

Ben Polcer from Manhattan

Playing on the street, that's how this whole thing happened. Before this, I was all over the place. All I was thinking about was what I wasn't getting done, how good I wasn't getting at the horn. When I came out here, all I had to think about was filling the air with my sound. You learn to simplify. Then, all the sudden, three months later you're like yeah, my chops are strong. Just by going out and playing music and not worrying about it.

Both my parents are jazz musicians. My father plays trumpet and my mother is a singer. One night she was filling in with his band. It was really snowy outside and she had left her amplifier in her car. My dad, the gentleman, offered to walk out and get it for her. So they had this romantic moment in the snow. She became very taken with him and started going to see him play at Eddie Condon's jazz club on West Fifty-fourth Street. One night they both sat down together during his set break, and my dad put his cigarette in the ashtray and turned it around so it pointed at my mother. That's how they fell in love.

After they got married, they both quit smoking and they ended

Ben sitting in with Tom Fischer's band at Fritzle's

up buying Eddie Condon's jazz club. It was a really old club, all kinds of people came there, Benny Goodman, Tony Bennett. Al Cohn used to hang out there. Now I play with his granddaughter Shaye Cohn in Loose Marbles. Six nights a week, my dad would play traditional jazz with his band. Being a kid, I don't think I really knew how lucky I was, but I'd just sit there and eat a hamburger or whatever and listen to this music. It was cool.

My parents never really forced music on me. When I was five they asked me if I wanted to take piano lessons. I was like, sure. They never made me practice, but every once in a while my mother would get me to sit down on the keys for five minutes, and if I didn't feel like it, I could stop. Then like an hour and a half later, I'd be like, whoa. What just happened? That was awesome.

When I was seven, I started playing trumpet. I'd play with my dad sometimes, but I took lessons from a guy named Allen Cohen. I used to go up to his dusty little storefront in midtown with rows of sheet music piled up to the ceiling. Upstairs, he had these really tiny practice rooms and you had some of the best musicians in the city in there. There I am, this seven year old kid playing scales on the trumpet and the next room over would be like the piano player for the

Letterman show.

When I went off to college, my parents were kind of wary about me being a music major. It's a hard life. Basically they just wanted me to be stable. Eventually they let me transfer to music school. I learned a lot about playing music, but nobody taught you how to survive as a musician. In 2005, I got hired as a director for a sports camp.

Just before I got that job, I'd met Michael Magro playing music in Washington Square Park. He had come up with name Loose Marbles when he was playing in Providence. It was the same kind of music I heard growing up, but it was grittier, and at the same time it also had this kind of sanctified feel, like church music. I was like damn I wanna do that. It's like when I met Michael, I found my identity. When I wasn't working, I'd go down to the park and we'd play. Pretty soon we started making decent money.

So there I was, looking out the window at work and it was a beautiful October day, and all I was thinking about was that I could totally be in Washington Square Park right now. We were getting offers to travel next summer, and I was gonna have to turn them down, because of this job. I had health insurance. I had a great salary — all this shit. And my parents were finally glad that I was stable. After a couple of days of mulling it over I was like man, I can't do this. I can't miss this chance. So I quit.

All that fall we played the park, and when it started getting cold we went into the subway. One day Michael just came up with the idea to pack up and come to New Orleans. I think in the back of our minds we figured we'd be back in New York by spring. We had no idea what was gonna happen.

I remember the first time we played down here. It just felt right. We were walking down Decatur Street and Michael saw these two kids that he knew from the subway in New York. We all headed down to the A&P to busk, and then more musicians started showing up, and like instantly Loose Marbles was a full band.

I've never played anywhere where this kind of music is so unanimously liked. On the street in New Orleans, it's not like you're just playing in a bar for people who wanna drink, you play for everybody. That's what they come here for. In other cities people have this misconception of jazz where they think it's this serious intellectual

Michael Magro

thing where you're supposed to just sit and watch, but out here people really get into it. It's pop music. Pop music is really just music that makes people dance. Eventually we got our own dancers. When Amy and Chance came in, it really opened up a whole new audience for us.

Most of our songs are only like three or four chords. It's actually really simple, but within that structure there's total freedom to improvise. You don't need to be a classically trained musician to understand it, so we play with people from all types of backgrounds. Some of us are second generation, third generation musicians and then some of us learned how to play going from city to city playing on the streets.

Probably the hardest part of what Michael and I do is having to decide who gets to play. We give everybody a chance for sure, but it would be impossible to just let anyone play with us whenever they want. We've made a lot of mistakes and we pissed a lot of people off. It's hard, because the street is the street. It's not like a gig. You don't own it. Sometimes personalities clash or styles clash. People aren't always dependable. It's not so much that it's about the money, but this really is our job and we all depend on each other. Like if a bass player doesn't show up, that hurts everybody. You have to make the group function. As much as it sounds ridiculous and it's just this street band, it's how we survive.

One way we make the band work is to keep it from being a band. Every band that I've been in where they had a set bass player and a set singer or whatever has fallen apart, self destructed. Everybody wants to kill each other or the band gets stuck in a rut. With this project we have to keep it in flux so it's fresh. One day it's this person, one day it's that person. With this style of jazz, it's really easy for different people to step in. We've played with, god, it must be hundreds of different musicians. That's what keeps it evolving.

The only thing that really frustrates me about this city and what we're doing is that it doesn't get integrated. I mean these are all good musicians I'm playing with, and soulful, but yeah, it really surprises me how little we've integrated the band. Music is definitely way easier to integrate than anything else. If you're a good musician, you're a good musician, it doesn't matter what color you are. And all good musicians know that, but it's the young kids. We had this one time where we were

playing on Frenchman at night and there was a young black brass band playing down the street and about three or four of them came over to hear us. This trumpet player, he was probably about fifteen years old, started talking to me on the break and he was just like, "What is this?" He was completely enthralled. Like, "This is like the coolest music I've ever heard and I know nothing about it. Who should I listen to?" That was awesome. I just wished it happened more. The fact that there aren't young black musicians coming in and sitting in with us very often is disturbing to me.

I'm not really sure where Loose Marbles will be in the future. I don't even really think about it too much anymore. There's something about New Orleans where I just get so caught up in the moment. What will be will be, but I have the feeling that what we're doing right now is what we should be doing. If people only listen to this music on old records it's gonna die out, but by taking it out on the street, we're showing that it's still relevant today. I don't know, I kind of feel like it's our mission or something.

Yegor Romantsov from The Ukraine

The story of Debauche is a very sad story:

There were only two of us left on the float (my Uncle Milan and I) when the Soviet nuclear submarine "Vodka Dva" ("Vodka Two" — English) or Vodka Vodka or lodochka podvodochka, as we use to call it with love, sunk in the Caribbean Sea after colliding with Cuban shrimping boat.... For two weeks me and my uncle Milan, whose two younger sisters were eaten by bears two weeks earlier (the most common death in the Ukraine — what a bad luck) were floating in the open seas with no drink and no water feeding on the carcass of a dead dolphin. Uncle Milan, the greatest milafonist of the Ukraine, suddenly felt sick. He never made it to the shore, holding his precious milafone until his last breath. He died of food poisoning (as doctors told me later.)

Finally, we were rescued, me and my dead uncle Milan, by Russian Mafia from Miami. They gave us shelter, food and had to beat up my uncle Milan only once for the bad smell. They put us to work. We had to wear high heels and pretend that we were women. They also taught us how to play musical instruments. I was playing a big drum, and my uncle Milan, who was still holding together, was playing his milafone.....

When we were first discovered as a band at the Seafood Festival by the greatest American anthropologist Conan O'brien, he made an astonishing analogy to our music: If Schwarzenegger and Chuck Norris (I like Chuck Norris personally) had to drink a lot of Vodka and have a lot of sex, that's what we sound like. Please enjoy it while we are here....*

When you grow up in a Soviet intelligentsia family they raise you like a samurai. You have to be good with the sword and you have to be good with the flute. When I was six my parents sent me to classical piano school where they make you sit at the piano for hours a day. If you didn't play right, the teacher would beat you up. I hated it. All I wanted was to play soccer. But then two years later, I closed my eyes and my fingers just started rolling over the keys. Just hands, no thinking. When I opened my eyes, I saw my fifty-six year old Russian teacher was in the corner crying.

When I turned thirteen, I picked up a guitar and started

* Transcription of secret CIA interrogation obtained by the editor under the Freedom of Intoxication Act

playing punk rock in a Young Pioneers castle. Everybody wore red silk scarves, and they were supposed to be teaching you about communism, but our supervisor was a really bad alcoholic, so he was happy we just made our own music and he could drink. It was a beautiful time to be a musician, because the USSR was falling apart and music was powering the movement.

At seventeen, I started a punk band called The Last Winter. I was just a little teenage cocksucker, so I didn't understand all the political aspects of what was going on, but basically my songs were calling for the end of communism. I could never say it outright, because KGB was everywhere. I didn't want to be like my grandfather who was sent to the gulag in Siberia. Basically we were shouting silence.

After Ukraine became its own country everything was fucking chaos. Money was worth nothing. I wanted to get out any way I could, so I got sexual asylum. I married an American teacher. It lasted three years.

When I got to America, it was a battle for survival. In Ukraine you can just be a fuckup and play music and drink and you can always find a bowl of borscht somewhere. Here you have to work. For ten years I was in California and New York, selling art, working like hell. I was like, what the fuck am I doing here? This is America, this is where everybody from Ukraine wants to be, but all I was doing was working and writing angry poetry and getting kicked out of bars. Three years ago I lost my place in New York so I moved to New Orleans.

I fell in love with this place because of grandmothers. People have grandmothers here like they have in Ukraine. If you don't have a grandmother, then you are an orphan. In New York, nobody has connections to the older generations, but here everything is connected to the past, especially the music. It made me think about the songs I had heard growing up, hooligan songs about jails and orphans and people getting killed. It's like Russian blues, like what your black folks were doing back in the days, music to transcend suffering.

All the time I was playing punk music, I was abandoning my culture, but when I started playing the old hooligan songs, I was embracing my past. People might not be able to understand the words, but they can feel where I come from. They know that I'm an orphan.

Debauche performing at the Dragon's Den

Hack Bartholomew from New Orleans

I grew up in Carrollton. It was mostly black people who worked for the rich people in the mansions on St. Charles Avenue. Back in the day, they used to call it nigger town, but with civil rights they started calling it the Black Pearl. When you think of black neighborhoods, you might picture yourself a ghetto, but it was middle class. It was a wonderful place to grow up.

My grandfather was pastor of Mount Moriah. Mahalia Jackson actually started singing there. At the time a lot of pastors were saying that Mahalia was singing the devil's music, because she had that blues influence. My grandfather was always behind her one hundred percent. She used to roll into town in a big old pink Cadillac and come have dinner with us. One time she sang at our church for a TV show with me in the choir backing her up. It was just overwhelming to be blessed so much. I'm telling you, from a child all the way up until now, God has taken care of me. Even when I was going left, he was always shaping me into going right.

Once I got older, I saw other people in the world doing their thing, and it looked like they were having so much fun. Cause sin is fun. I ain't gonna lie. The devil made sin fun so he could get you. When I turned twenty, I moved to New York thinking I was gonna make it big, and that's where I really got turned out.

I had me a little band called the Harlem Cowboys. We used to play club gigs, always hanging out with the hip crowd. Seems like I got to hang out with everybody who was somebody, Stevie Wonder, Boss Scaggs, Average White Band, George Benson. I even got to jam with the Rolling Stones one time in the studio. Thirteen years I spent in New York, but I never got that break. I wanted to do my own thing, get my own recognition, but God never let it happen. I started getting real hard into drinking and drugging, and things started falling apart.

One time, I went home to see my family and I got a girl pregnant. Back then we took care of our kids, so that was the end of me trying to be a superstar in New York. I got a few gigs around town, started working little jobs here and there. I was taking care of my kid, but any extra money went right to booze or drugs. I was a wreck.

40

A friend of mine was always trying to get me to go to church at Greater St. Stephen. I said, "I ain't going to no church and buying no preacher a Cadillac." But then he started talking about all the fine women with good jobs and pretty cars. My gigolo spirit took over. I was like, "Where's the church at?"

I wanted to look at all them women, so I sat way up in the balcony. When the choir started singing, that really hit me. I hadn't heard a gospel choir in years. I said, man this church is on! Bishop Martin up there, he started preaching about what it would profit a man to gain the whole world, but lose his soul. It was like he was talking straight at me.

At the end of the sermon Bishop Martin called out to the congregation for people who wanted to join the church. There must have been twenty people who walked up to that altar, but Bishop Martin said he wanted the whole church to pray, because he was waiting on just one more person battling and fighting the devil. I knew it was me. I wanted to get up, but the devil kept saying you ain't ready. You still smoking weed. You still doing cocaine. You still running around with different women. This church don't want people like you. They waited a good fifteen minutes. Then Bishop Martin starts, "I don't care what your problem is, what you're doing or what you done. God loves you just like you are. Come on!" I jumped up and started running to the altar, I was crying, snot coming down my nose. And that's where I came back to God.

Wanna know what really helped me get it back together? Joining the band. At the practice, the director, Dwight Franklin, he told me, what I want you to do is keep your horn behind your back, and then on the last song when I point to you, then you come out blowing. I tell you, when I busted out that horn at the service, that church went wild. Man, I'll tell you that's was something. Since then I been playing for Jesus.

Best gig I ever had.

Sam Young from New Orleans

I used to play rock and roll at these bars down here on Bourbon Street for the tourists. I tell you, that was some hard living. I was smoking two packs of cigarettes a day, drinking a case of beer a day, cocaine, marijuana — running behind women. The devil had me. I'd even died and come back. I was a mess. When I woke up in the morning, I just wanted to stay in bed. I didn't see no point in getting up and facing the world. It got to the point where I was just sick and tired of being sick and tired. Nine years ago, I turned my life over to Jesus.

God took the alcohol first and then the drugs and the cigarettes. I didn't wanna play on Bourbon Street no more, because I couldn't stand being around the smell, so I started playing with the band at church. I felt like a four-year-old kid, because for all that time I'd been dead. Now I'm alive. Everything is beautiful to me now.

A couple years ago, the Lord blessed me with a song, *Jesus is My Friend.* I was just strumming my guitar and his words came through me. That's not my song, that's God's song. When God gave me that gift, I felt like he was calling me to take his word out to the people on the streets.

I'm no preacher man, you don't see me shouting at the people passing by. I just let my music be a vessel for Jesus. He gave it to me and I'm gonna pass it on. I wanna see everybody feeling like this here. See what the rich people got, I'm richer. I got joy. They got people with all that money and they don't have what I got. You can't buy joy. You get that from the Lord. I'm telling you, man, if I had me some wings I would fly.

Sam Young

Willie Holmes from New Orleans

I been singing out here in front of the Café DuMonde since '94, but I didn't really start singing gospel until after Katrina. Before the storm I was singing mostly secular songs. I loved making the people smile, but honestly I was more worried about the money in the box than the music. Apparently, the NOPD had some issues with that approach, because on August 22nd, 2005, they arrested me up on Bourbon Street and charged me with panhandling. I understand that there's an eight o'clock curfew for performers on Bourbon, but I don't know why they had to charge me with panhandling, I'm not a bum. People like what I do.

I was supposed to only be locked up for a few days, but then when the storm started coming, they weren't letting anybody see the judge. When the water started coming in, all the officers panicked and locked us down in the cells and told us a bunch of lies and left the building. I was on the second floor, but they had some prisoners who were locked up down below and the water was starting to fill up. Some of the inmates broke free and they went into the gym and got the big goal posts and started banging them against the hydraulic doors. They were banging on those doors for hours until finally we broke the lock. If we didn't get those guys out, they would have drowned.

It's amazing how God put all the minds together in a time of trauma. It didn't matter who did something to you on the street, we were all working together to get those guys out. Once we got everybody out of the cells, we still stuck with no food and just a little water. We started hanging sheets out the windows and lighting them on fire to let the people know that we were still in there. When we were just about to run out of water, the Department of Corrections showed up in canoes and started evacuating people over to the bridge. Some of the guys were jumping out and swimming underwater, but I just had a little municipal charge, so there was no need to take that chance. Those officers said they were gonna shoot to kill.

At the bridge, they put me on a bus and evacuated me to Shreveport. I got a hold of my family over the phone, and thank God, everybody was alright. I guess that was the one time they were happy

to hear I was in jail. Everyday up in Shreveport I thought that I was gonna be getting out, but all the records had been destroyed in the flood, so it wasn't until December 8th that I finally got released. I was only supposed to be in jail for a week.

When I finally came back down to the Café DuMonde to sing, I wasn't the same person. The Lord had really touched me through Katrina. I'd seen all the baddest criminals in the city united together to save each other's lives and that really opened my eyes to God's love. On top of that, we had people coming from all over the world at their own expense to help rebuild this city. I felt the power of the Spirit and I just wanted to spread that love through gospel music, sharing his word through my voice.

"Grandpa" Elliott Small from New Orleans

"Elliott Small is a hell of a song writer. We laid some tracks. Oh yeah we used to lay some tracks. Elliott Small — hell of a songwriter."
— Dr. John

Grandpa say French Quarter ain't making no money today. When they had ships lined up on the river for three miles on every side, French Quarter was making money. When the ladies of the night walking up and down on high heels, some had wigs, some had their own hair, looked just as beautiful. I was out there. French Quarters was making money.

Sometimes a person can hurt somebody and not know it.

Don't get me wrong, I'm a man amongst men and there's no girly in me. But I'm happy to say, I love all women. But there's a but to it. Sometime a man can be wrong and a woman can be wrong too. What I mean by, I don't mean no harm, but for to make a man happy buy him a car, a set of shotguns, name brand shotguns, a set of name brand shotguns and a boat and a man is very happy.

What make a woman happier than a man and happier than ever, now this is some ladies, it's not the majority. I don't mean no harm ladies. I still love you all just the same. But it's not the material thing that will make a woman happy. You give her a diamond jewelry she won't be as happy as for a man to pick a rose off a tree and give it to her. I done seen it. *

I grew up on Orleans Avenue in the Treme. When I was a little bitty boy one day my uncle ran out the house and left his harmonica sitting on the kitchen table. That was it. It was on. It didn't take me but five minutes till I put that thing in my mouth, stuck it in there upside down. To this day that's still the way I play.

Used to play along to my mother's radio. That radio was my best friend. She used to put it way up on the top shelf, where I couldn't reach the dial. She loved her classical music, so that's what I played. Imagine how it sounded, little six year old boy trying to keep up with Mozart on harmonica? Yeah buddy. I caught enough beatings making noise with this thing. Then one day my mama washing clothes in the scrub bowl and she started singing "If I Love You." I put that harmonica

* unedited

48

"Grandpa" Elliott Small

to my lips and I started playing along. She ran out the bathroom. She was shocked. She said do it again, play it again, do it again. My momma loved that song. From that day on, I didn't catch no more hell for playing this harmonica.

My momma, she saw I was something special, she knew I was gonna be a entertainer. She put me in front the television and I watched Fred Astaire do his stunts. I learned how to tap dance right there in front of that TV. Upper pose, backwards flip, into a spit, come back up, forward split, forward flip into a split, tapping in cadence like a drum, yeah buddy. And I was doing all this while I was playing the harmonica. My momma bought me a set of real taps and took me out to Bourbon Street.

I wasn't like the kids today with the tin cans on they shoes, shuffling they feet for a few seconds and then running up to the tourists with they box. That ain't tapping, that's begging. I was doing real tapping. Had me different color suits, white on white, red on red, black on black with a coat tail, shoes sparkling. I could show you pictures, but they all got washed away.

When I was seven a man saw me tapping down on Bourbon and he wanted to take me up to New York to be in a Broadway show. Me and my momma moved into the East Bronx. They had me in *Old Man River* and *Showboat*. I used to tap dance with the other dancers, and then I'd play my harmonica right out front with the orchestra.

I loved being on that stage, but being in that house was hell. My mother had settled in with this other man, and he used to beat her and he used to beat me. If I was five minutes late coming home from school, I got a beating. Took all my clothes off and had me in handcuffs and was just beating me up. I told my momma that she should pack up and just leave, but this man said I didn't have no business telling grown folk how to act. I just caught more beatings.

He killed my mother.

He crashed the car, and she died right there. I've never told anyone that for years. We took the body back to New Orleans for the funeral at Mount Carmel Baptist Church, my great great grandfather's church, name was Reverend G.M. Taylor.

After that I went with my grandmother. She was a kind hearted old lady. I used to come home every night with a big bucket full of quarters from tapping and give it to her. I always had to take the bus home, because back in those days, black folks couldn't ride in no taxi. The only way black folks were even allowed in the Quarters was if you had a chef hat on your head or taps on your feet.

Tenth grade I dropped out of McDonogh 45 and started going down to the river doing long shore work when they let me. It would be real hard unloading and loading the boats. Aaron Neville used to be in one ship hole and I used to be in another ship hole and we'd be down there loading the barrels and singing. Sung my can off.

When I was seventeen, I got hurt on the ship and messed up my knee real bad, so I couldn't tap dance no more, so I came out here singing. Guy by the name of Joe Broussard, he found me in the Quarter, and he said I had a good recording voice. We sat down to write some songs.

Back then I used to wear my hair all the way down my back, a permanent, cold black. My face was like a baby. All the girls used to fall for me. They used to say that boy's a devil, ain't no way that boy's gonna be a Christian. We got to talking about that and we came up with the song "I'm a Devil." We took it to Wardell Quezergue and he arranged it and recorded it. Put it out on Bang Records.

There was a disk jockey at BOK, and he took a liking to me, because I had big arms from working on the ships. He was that way. I brought the record up there, and he threw it on the turntable and said I'm gonna break this. It was a fantasy thing for him, trying to get in my corner, so one day he could proposition me. I didn't play that. But man, he got that record out there. Yeah buddy. Seemed like "I'm a Devil" was the only one they was playing.

I went on tour locally with that. Played on the same stage as Fats Domino did when he had his big record, *They Call me the Fat Man*. I came out in a suit, red on red, red socks, red shoes, big pitchfork in my hand. Background girls dressed as imps. When I sang, "I'm a Devil" They pointed at me singing, "He's the booger man."

It's been so long, I almost forgot it.

"I'm a Devil" was a hit, but one thing you gotta understand about New Orleans and the music business is that everybody's crooked. They took my song and gave it to this other band Satan and Satan's Roses. I seen 'em at the Gonga Den, sounded terrible. They put my song on a record and didn't even put my name on it. Never saw a penny.

I'm a hell of a songwriter, but mostly I was a stylist, teaching people how to sing. Used to always be down in the Lower Ninth Ward at Joe Broussard's house. They called it The Shack. Just a little bitty house with no food in the fridge, everybody's stomachs growling and we would sit there and write. Gene Knight, "Mr. Big Stuff" came out that house. King Floyd, "Groove Me." I helped write a bunch of King Floyd's shit, but he never gave me the credit. If it wasn't for me, "Barefootin'" wouldn't have been a hit. Wardell Quezergue had recorded it and then put it in the can, I listened to it and said, damn, that's a hit. Ended up selling twenty million copies. The Dixie Cups, I'm the cause of them getting their break, because I was the one who told Joe Jones to bring them up to New York. Al Green, I told this manager about him. He wanted me but I was under contract. Couple years later I heard, "I'm so tired of being alone, I'm so tired upon..." Yeah buddy.

1969, I came out with my second album *Girls are Made for Loving*. One night I saw a guy and he was beating up on this lady. I threw him up against the wall, that ain't the way to treat a lady. Girls were made to be loved not beat on. Went home and I wrote that song. I wanted that Motown sound and I got it. It was a hit. They had me touring all through the south with that. When I played in Texas, I looked out in the audience and it was nothing but white faces.

I kept writing more hits, but the record companies stopped getting behind me. When Dr. John was out in California I wrote a song for him called "Evil Knievel." He paid me, but they never released it. 1976 I had a funk record called *E-Ni-Me-Ni-Mi-Ni-Mo* with the same musicians that played for King Floyd. That never broke. My last record was in 1986, *Gotta be Serious*. The producer, Isaac Bolden, he didn't even release it, he just wanted to trick me to get the rights to my music. He made me sign a contract, and he slid another piece of paper in there that gave all my shit to him. All my royalties, that all goes to him, that motherfucker. I need to get a lawyer, because I gotta get what's due to me before I die.

I'm a Katrina child and I don't have a penny.

To look at me, you'd think I'm not just shit, but the things I did, people who I helped, they still helping theyself. All that helping to

record, helping to rehearse, helping to write and play, all of 'em said if I get a hit you won't have nothing to worry about. Nobody gave me shit. Makes me bitter. Makes me mad, makes me angry.

I just said y'all can go to hell. I'm gonna just come out hard on the street. 'Cause out here it ain't nothing but music. Can't nobody outdo my name on these streets. I put it in the people's mind to come down to New Orleans and live forever. You know how many people done told me I'm the reason they moved here? I'm better than a stimulus package.

Came out here and met a blues man, Stoney B, grandson of Howling Wolf. Stoney the one who started calling me Grandpa, had that name ever since. We put a mark on this town. It's like we got the same mind. We don't even have to rehearse. We just didn't play, we put on a show. You see these overalls and this hat, that ain't my real clothes, that's a costume. We play like we were a bunch of hicks from out the boonies, but it ain't nothing but a joke to get the tourists to laugh. I played the role of a crazy blind man. Used to act a fool.

All these years I was just playing the role of a blind man, but then all the sudden I started losing my sight. Lost my whole left eye and now I got nothing but a little window in my right. Everyday it's getting smaller. Pretty soon, it's gonna be totally dark. But being blind I love music even more, because eyes really is music. The scenery, beautiful things, pretty things.

I done lost all track of time I been out here so long, but when I'm in the French Quarters I be so free nothing worries me. All I wanna do is keep a smile on people's faces. Singing my heart out in the cold, in the sleet, in the rain. I think of all them folks that made it big all the time, playing stadiums, theaters. But look, the French Quarter ain't got no roof. My concert hall is as far as the eye can see. This is my home. This is where I belong. You'd have to put a shackle on this arm, put a shackle on that arm and get a whole team of horses to pull me out of here.

Editor's Note: Grandpa is featured in the documentary film Playing for Change. *On March 23rd, 2009, he performed on the* Tonight Show *with musicians from all around the globe.*

Peter Bennett from Virgil, New York

It is a glass harmonica, young fellow. Twenty-six water tuned goblets forming a chromatically tuned instrument that spans two octaves and a major second. What tune would you folks like to hear on this glass harmonica? Come on folks, challenge me, name a tune I don't know. Where are you from sir? Tennessee? Perhaps you'll recognize this tune. "The Tennessee Waltz" is the name of that melody. Dancing is encouraged. Big dip now. Oh nobody's dancing?

Sir, thank you for your kind donation.

I've been playing here on the streets of New Orleans since the early nineties, but it seems I've been playing with glass all my life. Sir, I have vague recollections of fifty odd years ago, some of them very odd years indeed, getting in trouble at Sunday dinner for messing with my water glass. I figure in a very real sense I've been getting in trouble messing with glass ever since.

Now it did take me two years to collect this set of goblets. I had to audition over two thousand pieces of glass to build the instrument, and although young fellow, I certainly don't recommend it, I DID HAVE TO DRINK A POWERFUL AMOUNT TO GET THEM ALL, I FEAR!

They are all just common ordinary bar glasses. This glass came from my late mother's china cabinet. This glass came from the Salvation Army at Key West, Florida. This glass came from Smitty Restaurant Supply in Syracuse, New York. So you can see each of these glasses has a story all of its own. Unfortunately, there are all kinds of reasons that glasses get changed from time to time, breakage not the least of them. One night I did have a young fellow who was kind of off his rocker hurl himself at me from behind and dropped the instrument on the deck. Much to my amazement it broke no glass at all.

I am something of a fanatic about talking to people when I play, especially when there are so few of them out on the street. That is one of the first things that I discovered when I took this instrument on the road. It's not good enough to be a virtuoso on your instrument, and I'm certainly not a virtuoso. People want to be entertained.

I'm part of a small but very active community of glass musicians in the world. Out of forty serious players, there are only three of us who are stupid enough to try and earn a living at it. We try to get together once every three or four years. The last time was in 2005, when I was invited to perform in Paris at Le Cite de la Music. Over the course of a lovely evening, it turned out that I am far from the best glass player in the world, but I'm a hell of a lot better entertainer than any of the rest of them are.

Big Mamma Sunshine from Walden County, Florida

How we doing good people? Big Mamma Sunshine! Your antique musician. Hooo! Look at 'em a strutting here. Well wooeee, we got Miss Sugar. Hello, Sugar Booger. Shake it, mamma!

I'm a country woman. Grew up in one of them itty-bitty towns where you blink when you go by on the highway. When I was a little girl, my mamma said I could either learn to crochet or play the piano. I tried to learn a chain stitch, but I didn't have the patience. I'm not no homemaker. Ha Ha Ha! Oh no! I'm an old maid. That's what I am. But you better watch out cause we wild women don't get the blues!

My mamma couldn't afford piano lessons, so she put me in front of that radio and I learned to play the blues. Well word got 'round, and people come and start setting on my porch to listen. We was in a dry county and nobody had any place to go. When somebody'd get a new piano and they'd come get Big Mamma to play it. I played for lots of people, but it was always just ladies having cake and coffee. If you messed with the menfolk then you were fixing for trouble.

When the good old boys got to drinking there was liable to be a commotion. I remember one night my daddy was standing in a big circle of people holding his knife and my mamma sent me in to stop the fight. I coulda got cut. I saw a lotta women that did. I never did get along too good with my daddy. It hurt me real bad, the way he'd do me.

I never thought of getting paid to play the piano, because women weren't considered musicians, we just played at home. I made my grocery money washing dishes, then when my mamma got sick I took over for her at her beauty parlor. Did that for a many years.

In 1988, I got real sick and wound up in the hospital. Doctor ended up taking away my driver's license away 'cause my health. I was thinking what I outta do for myself cause they ain't got no busses in Walden County, so I say, I'm gonna go down to New Orleans and be a troubadour of the trails. I been playing out here ever since.

Now I'm three years working on seventy. I got both feet on the breaks and going just as hard as I can. Ha ha. Everybody's going along with me. So, well I guess that's all that counts. It puts the biscuits on the table. Big Momma's gonna keep socking it to the rocket.

Now grab that tambourine and do the wham bam doodle!

Roger Cornish from New Orleans

I've never considered this home. This was the place where I was raised, so it is home in one sense. But my true home is my soul, my spirit. As long as I can stay in touch with that, I'm home. Because when you leave this place, your soul is the only thing you take with you.

Growing up I always thought I'd be an astronaut, explore the universe, step beyond the boundaries of the Earth. It really broke my heart when I found out that I was too tall. Then in '85 I heard Coltrane's *Love Supreme* on WWOZ. I was like wow, this cat is out there, like in a whole different universe. That saxophone was like his rocket ship, but it wasn't going to outer space, it was going to inner space, reaching into the depths of his soul. Once I got hit by the Trane, that was it. I guess you could say that I became a spiritual astronaut, out to explore my own universe.

Growing up in the Twelfth Ward, of course I listened to a lot of the traditional New Orleans music — Louis Armstrong, the different brass bands. I have tremendous respect for those performers, but to me it always seemed like their music was more about entertainment, playing for other people. When I heard bop, it hit me as being more free, not having to worry about fitting into a particular niche that society defined for it. With bop there's no rules, no schedule, it's an unlimited opportunity to express the mysticism of the mind.

Before I started playing sax, I was a martial arts instructor, working with some of the best kick boxers in the world. That same discipline just transferred over into my music. When I first started, I used to play for twelve hours a day. After a while, it got to the point that I figured I might as well take it out on the street. At first I used to be affected by the fact that I wasn't always appreciated, but after a while I realized that if I just meditated and tuned into the music, the money in the case would take care of itself. See, it's a love thing. It's my worship, my offering to the universe — to God.

There was a time in my life when music was the only thing that mattered to me. As I get older, my responsibilities are starting to play a bigger part. Just before Katrina, my wife and I brought a beautiful son into the world, so at times I've had to put down my horn and work

some jobs to make ends meet. Right after the storm was a real struggle, because there were no tourists out here. FEMA paid three months of my rent, and then I had to start living in my van, because I couldn't find another place. My wife and son are staying with her family. I still see them everyday, but it's still hard to not have that comfort of having our own home. It's been a struggle.

The other day I was out here playing and this little kid came up to me and told me that he'd lost his family. I don't know why he chose me. I guess there must have been some spiritual connection. God comes in a lot of forms. I asked him if there was anybody he could call and he said no. I asked if there was anything I could do for him, but he just wanted to keep searching. When he was gone, I just started crying — a grown man crying. I think it was because I realized that his world was lost. It wasn't so much the sadness, it was the compassion. I was feeling this deep love inside my soul, and it came out through tears.

Then I picked up my horn and started to play.

Bilal Sunni Ali from Harlem

When I was a senior in high school, I did a paper on the similarities between Malcolm X and John Coltrane. Those were two very different cats, but they were both very focused on self-determination. Malcolm was dealing with it politically, controlling the apparatus that governed his life, and Trane was dealing with it culturally, taking control of the apparatus that governed his art. Throughout my life, I always saw myself playing the roles of both of those cats as a revolutionary.

Being a musician in New York, we all felt this sense of power, because you had a lot of street gangs, but as musicians we were recognized as like a neutral force. Whatever neighborhood we were from, it was cool to go somewhere else and play. We broke down the barriers between blacks and Latins, bringing oppressed people together. My dad came from the Garafuna people in Honduras, so I was indisputably a link between those two cultures.

My family had converted to Islam, so I spent a lot of time with the Sankore Nubian Cultural Society, which was led by Salah al Din Shakur. That's the family where Tupac got his name. They basically taught us about the African traditions and celebrated black culture. When I was 18, I joined the Black Panthers.

Music was the soul of the movement. It's like a transmission of energy and intelligent understanding that words can't develop. It wasn't so much the virtuosity as it was the place where the music was coming from, a reflection of the struggle. I remember when I first heard Pharaoh Sanders, it just hit me as a growling sound that just expressed the anger of the day, the feeling of contempt for the society that perpetuated such ills on people.

I played with all sorts of cats: Pharaoh, Yusef Lateef, The Last Poets. Over the years I've spent a lot of time playing with Gill Scott Heron.* I had actually gone to middle school with Gill, so we were both coming from the same place in terms of our inspiration. As a writer, Gill was communicating on the intellectual level and the musicians got behind him on the emotional level. The movement and the music were inseparable. By me being both a Black Panther and musician, I was like an ambassador for the movement.

* Bilal is featured on the albums: *It's Your World, The First Minute of a New Day, From South Africa to South Carolina*

By the late sixties, Panther groups started moving in different directions. There were a lot of things going on on the West Coast that we didn't agree with or didn't understand. They sent me over to Berkeley to get a better concept of what was going on. One day the police came to my apartment. They were actually looking for another guy, but they searched the place and found two cans of gunpowder. Legally you were only allowed to have one. I pled guilty, because they said I wouldn't have to do that much time. That was a mistake, because I ended up dong three and a half years in Soledad.

The movement had really changed when I was released. Panthers were killing Panthers, relatives of mine killed friends of mine. It still makes me angry that as enlightened as we were, we fell for such traps as to begin killing each other to prove a point. We had more key organizers that were dead or in jail than on the street.

In 1976, I married my wife Fulani and we started a family. That really started to change my revolutionary philosophy. When you're a teenager, you want everything to be immediately gratifying, like, let's knock out this regime and run this bad boy. But having children made me start thinking more long term. The philosophy is just as radical, but it's more focused on education and transforming people's minds, hopefully without hurting anybody.

I still considered myself a Panther, but Fulani and I had also become involved with the Republic of New Afrika. Our goal was to transform the Black Belt South into a liberated zone with a government controlled by black people. New Orleans was the capital. In 1978 we moved here to lay down the foundations for the provisional government. In some ways New Orleans was more like home than New York, because black culture has deeper roots here. A lot of my family was living here, so it was good to be raising our children around family.

As the Republic of New Afrika began to grow, the government started to fabricate charges against us to try to bring us down. Because of my associations, I was accused of being involved with the Brinks armored car robbery in New York. I'd already experienced how the legal system abuses black people in the United States, so I went into exile in Belize. They captured me there and brought me back to stand trial.

My attorney was Chowke Lumumba and the DA was Rudy Giuliani. Lumumba was brilliant. He made it clear that I was being targeted because of my politics and not because I had done anything wrong. At the end of our closing arguments, we played a recording of *The Liberation Song* that I had recorded with Gill. We won.

I'm still a conscious citizen of the Republic of New Afrika, but since Katrina my wife and I have been working on establishing a music clinic in Punta Gorda, Belize through the Universal Negro Improvement Association. Our goals are basically the same as they were for the Black Panthers, lifting up the community by celebrating black culture. The government in Belize is actually willing to work with us, so there's no need to rebel against them in a violent way. A lot of New Orleans musicians who got displaced by Katrina are getting involved with the project. We plan on putting together a brass band for the school down there.

For the past few weeks, I've been staying in New Orleans, because I just finished playing at the Black Panther Reunion in Atlanta, and I'm supposed to play another gig in Texas in a few weeks. I lined up a few club gigs in town, but as a Muslim I feel like a hypocrite getting paid for encouraging people to drink. Basically, I've just been hitting the streets so I can send back money to Belize to pay for instruments. Come January, I'll be down there teaching. I know that I'm going to miss New Orleans, but I'm excited to take what I've learned here and share it with the world.

Editor's Note: Visit Sidewalksaints.com for links to Bilal's reflections on his experiences with young Tupac Shakur.

George Blackmon from New Orleans

When I play this here, I ain't bragging on myself and I ain't boasting, but to me, I think I'm a ten out of ten. When I go out on Canal and put my buckets over the grates, that sound goes underground for ten blocks and I got people walking miles to come hear where it coming from. I'm the sound of New Orleans. I'm telling you bro, I get funky on this here. But I thank God first, because this ain't me, it's the God in me that makes me play.

I picked up my first pair of drumsticks when I was seven years old. My momma played organ at the church and my daddy was a drummer too, so it's in my blood. But what really got me going was playing in the marching band at Dunbar Elementary. My band teacher, Mr. Melvin Washington, I was his best student. I remember right before we was gonna play at the Poseidon Parade on the West Bank, Mr. Washington's daddy died and he had to go to the funeral. He took me into his office and he handed me the bell chase, and he said he wanted me to lead the band. So there I was, a little twelve-year-old boy, leading the whole band. We came in second place. I felted good that day. I'll never forget it.

Coming out of school, I was playing drums in a band. We never made it big and I got to the point where I was feeling depressed, ain't loved and ain't wanted. Pretty soon drugs started getting in the way, and I wasn't focused on my music anymore. I wasted years of my life trying to go into programs, but each time I got out, I'd go back to the same thing. When Katrina hit, I was living at my mother's house and going to a program called Jesus of Miracle Power.

I evacuated to Sulphur Springs, Texas, and that's where I met my wife, Audrey. I lost a lot in that storm, but it weren't for Katrina, I never would have met my wife. It was beautiful being a part of her family, but pretty soon I was going back to my old ways. I guess I still had New Orleans in the back of my mind. Audrey couldn't take it anymore, so a year ago I decided I wanted to come back home.

At first, I was thinking maybe I could get me a little job, but the Mexicans done got all the jobs, so I ended up going down underneath that bridge over the I-10. That bridge was wild, bro, drug

George Blackmon

infested and everything. Being in that world you gotta have some sort of hustle. I ain't into robbing people or stealing from people, so that's when I found me some buckets and started taking 'em down to Canal Street to make me some money. It was good to be back to making my music, but my friends was always saying lets go get high, lets go get high. It felt like my music was destroying me.

Thank God the city cleaned up that bridge, because that wasn't a place for nobody. Once I got myself outta there, I started realizing what kind a hurt I was putting on my family. I got on the phone and I called Audrey and told her how much I loved her. She said that if I could get my life together and get off a them drugs, that I could come back home to Texas. I got off that phone and I got down on my knees and thanked the Lord that she still had it in her heart to take me back.

Right now, I got two months, eight days, and, let me see what time it is, eight hours clean. I'm renting me a little room, and I call Audrey every day so I can stay focused. I know I'm gonna get her back, but it ain't easy because the temptation is out here. When it get on my mind, I stop in the middle of the street, it don't matter where I am, because I ain't ashamed a nobody, and I get on my knees and I pray right there where I'm at. Before I get off my knees and walk to the next corner that urge is gone.

In my future I feel that God gonna prosper me. When God give me back my wife, I could see a whole lot further. Like they say, once you was blind, now you can see. Now I can see. Today I can see that my wife completes me. I don't want my wife, I need my wife. When I have my wife, you ain't gonna see me on these streets no more.

Editor's Note: George called a month later from Texas. He and Audrey sat together in front of the computer and watched a video I had recorded of George singing a song dedicated to his family.

Gonzo from St. Louis

Everybody has a beat. The first nine months of your life, all you hear is duh dut, duh dut. We've all got rhythm, even white people who think they don't. It's like a baby, you just have to feed it and it will grow. Like me, six months ago I never thought I'd be playing the drums on the street. Then I got stranded in Indianapolis, dead broke, I saw a kid banging on his drum and I decided to give it a shot.

Since then I've been all around the country. I play for eight to twelve hours a day and I never go hungry. I get to meet thousands of everybodies — rich kids, broke kids, gutter punks, businessmen. I get to make little kids and their sixty-five year-old grandmothers dance their ass off. My favorite is letting little kids beat on my drum. I teach 'em how to play and then their parents give me money.

My family thinks I'm nuts. They say I should go to school for heating and air so I can get a real job. They say I'm not getting my hands dirty. Look at my hands. My calluses are thicker than a goddamn steel worker. It's a fucking job. Spring break in Florida I can make a G a week. Tonight, I might make eight bucks, but it's not about the money. Its about the beat. If I don't play for a couple days I feel weird.

Basically, I'm getting ready for the apocalypse. God forbid, in 2012, when the empire crumbles and this country is bombed to fuck, there's gonna be no radio, no TV, no fucking American Idol. It's already happening. Pretty soon, it's gonna be like back in the caveman days when we made music by banging on rocks. I'm gonna be ready.

Gonzo

Robin Attwood from Forest Park, Washington

It's like casting spells, like starting a bloody fire. Oh my God, it's really like I'm hooked up to heaven when I play washboard. It's just beats within beats within beats. Whoosh whoosh whoosh. It's so bloody awful. Sometimes I hit the lamp posts. Last night I was pressing all the buttons on this broken telephone making change come out while I was playing. Oh it's great. It's a royal safari, the washboard is.

I guess I'd have to say my childhood was pretty genial. My family was all lovey-dovey. Right now, they worry about me a lot while I'm traveling. I don't always tell them what I'm doing, but I still love them to bitsies. Which is funny, because it seems that with a lot of traveling kids, they don't think you're cool unless you've had a miserable childhood. It's like you can't be legit unless you had to suffer.

Growing up, I wasn't miserable, but it always seemed like I was separated from myself, very bored but very anxious. I couldn't wait for anything. One day, I was walking down the interstate with my ukulele, and there was this little crest in the road where I could balance myself on one foot. So I was standing there balancing, and then I felt this feeling in my flesh, this hyper awareness. It was the grandest of epiphanies — the essence of the moment. I realized that I was thinking about thinking. Then I started thinking about thinking about thinking and all that jazz. I just about fell off my feet. Christ my name is Robin, that's what people say, but I realized I don't know anything about what's going on in this moment. Nothing. It was like having the realization that you're born a marionette and then you cut your strings and you walk around and find things to attach yourself to.

That's when I first started keeping my journals. Everyday, I write for three hours, trying to make sense of it all. When I go back to visit my parents, I put five or six notebooks in a drawer and leave them there. It's like my own history.

I guess playing on the street is kind of like my nine to five, a way to support my writing. Hopefully, I'll be able to go somewhere with my stories. I just wanna see if it's worth it at all. Otherwise I think I might as well be this dirty man in the gutter.

Dougie the Squatter Pimp from Detroit

Excuse me, sir, can you spare some change for a song? Anything helps. Change? Thanks have a good night.

My mom was a crackhead 'til I was four, then she tried to kill herself so I moved in with my grandparents and it was real chill 'til I was ten, then I lived with my dad 'til I was fourteen and he kicked me out. I dyed my hair black and he called me a faggot so I pushed him. I was already on probation, so I violated and had to go to juvie, then I got out and got kicked out of high school, so I just left home and started hitchhiking and jumping freights. My childhood affected me a lot. I grew up around a lot of drugs. I do a lot of drugs. I grew up poor. I'm still poor. It's alright though, it's what made me — me.

I talk to my dad on and off. He's an asshole. He wouldn't accept my calls last time I ended up in jail. My mother's fine now. She's a born again Christian. I didn't talk to her for a long time, but now that I'm a grown ass man, I call her. She's still as poor as I am, still on SSI. I call her to let her know I'm alive. She thinks I go to jail a bit too much, and I do.

Flying a sign is my most solid hustle. Today I made a hundred dollars in two hours uptown. I'd rather play music, but if I gotta get that money, I'll get that money. It's stupid, because you think people would rather hear some music, but it's been true everywhere I go, you make more money panhandling. You just can't do it in the same spot all the time or else the cops kick you out.

In the Quarter you've gotta play music or the cops will bust you. I just jam out and freestyle and ask people if they want to hear a song. Sometimes other street musicians get pissed off at me, because they say I should just be playing. I'd rather try to get someone to stop, because then I know they're at least going to give me a dollar. A few weeks ago, I got a hundred dollar kick down for one song. That's why it's better to get people to stop and listen, because then you can tell 'em what's going on with yourself. People understand. Anybody who's fucking partly human should have a little bit of compassion for someone like me.

Dougie the Squatter Pimp

Clarence Gallagher from Tacoma

I got my first guitar when I was eleven-years-old. I'm eighteen now, so I guess I been playing this thing for seven years. My grandmother gave it to me for Christmas. She used to be a singer in a psychedelic band back in the sixties, went to Woodstock and everything. She actually showed me some old tabs of acid that she keeps with her old albums. Grandma definitely formed my musical world. I started teaching myself guitar with her old records.

I'll never forget hearing "Traveling Riverside Blues" on *Led Zeppelin II*. That song just about put me on the floor. I was like, who is this Robert Johnson character? I just started downloading all of his songs and figuring them out. It felt kind of weird to be learning how to play this old music clicking on a mouse and staring at a computer screen, but it was just so easy. It was like being in the biggest record store in the world and being able to have anything I wanted.

When I really started getting into the blues, I used to cut out of school and go back in the woods and play guitar all day long. In school I was always bored, but out there in the forest I felt like I was really learning something. Once in a while a teacher would call my house, but things were pretty crazy at home, so I could do whatever I wanted.

When I hit sixteen, I knew I had to leave home. My stepfather wasn't really a good guy, so it was hard to watch him around my mom. I got a couple suitcases, my record player and guitar and just walked out the door and went to stay with my girlfriend.

Kaylee and I actually met back when I was in seventh grade. We'd been real good friends for a few years. Then one night we were tripping on mushrooms and we ended up sitting together in the back of her friend's car. I looked over and saw that long curly hair and those big blue eyes and I guess something just kinda clicked. I put my arm around her shoulder and that was it. I'd never felt that way before. We've been together ever since.

We were doing all right in Tacoma. I was helping my dad with some plumbing and Kaylee had a job painting cars. It was good, but deep down I was itching to get out of Washington. That summer we went out traveling and we wound up passing through New Orleans. I

Clarence Gallagher

took my guitar out on Royal Street and as soon as I started strumming, it was like I could feel all those old blues players in the wind. A bunch of people came by and started dancing and clapping. By the end of the night I looked down and saw that there must have been forty or fifty dollars in the case. It was so amazing. I was used to unclogging shit from out of toilets, and here I was getting paid for something I like doing. I didn't wanna leave. Kaylee and I made up our minds that as soon as we could save up enough money in Tacoma we were gonna move down here.

So that's what we did.

When we rolled into town two months ago, we were sleeping at night in our car. Within two weeks we had our own studio apartment. I'd picked up a washboard for Kaylee back in Tacoma, so now she plays with me. She helps out a lot, it's a much fuller sound. Plus I think people tip more when they see a pretty girl. We're together just about all the time. I think it's really made us stronger. We're still just as much in love if not more. Last week I wrote a song about her called *I Got a Gal*. "I got a gal, love her so. Call her my sweet jelly roll."

The other street musicians have been real kind, showing us the ropes about what songs to play and where the best spots are at. Little tricks, like wearing nice clothes so that I look professional and approachable. Everybody always gets excited because we're so young. They always seem tickled when they find out I'm just eighteen. I guess I don't feel like I'm eighteen because I've been out fending for myself for so long.

It's definitely a struggle sometimes. It's hard to come up with money for rent and still have enough money for food. We just applied for food stamps to help us out with that. But all in all, I can't complain. I'm out here playing the music I love, with the woman I love. I'm not sure where it's gonna take me, but right now I wake up every morning and love being where I'm at.

Mad Mike the Hippie Bum from New Orleans

GIVE ME SOME MONEY SO I CAN BUY DRUGS!
GIVE ME SOME MONEY SO I CAN BUY DRUGS!

When somebody comes walking down the street, I have ten seconds to get their attention. Every line out of my mouth has to be a hook, something to make them smile. I could be composing *Rhapsody in Blue* right here on this sidewalk, and people would not give a fuck. Making money off music is a fundamentally different process than making music for the sake of music. I'm not really looking for money to buy drugs, at least not right now, but I am pretty broke tonight, so that's the approach that I've gotta take.

I grew up in New Orleans, man. My parents were total right wing Christians, very anti-free thought, very Republican — totally adverse to the whole New Orleans vibe. When I was ten, we moved away. Then at seventeen I left home and became a homeless bum. I ended up hitchhiking down here, and when I hit the Quarter, all the sudden I felt like I was back home. I think what turned me on was that my parents hated this place so much — pure teenage rebellion.

The Quarter seemed like Shangri-la, man. Like one block away could be a whole other world, limitless possibilities. When I realized that it was possible to survive just by playing my guitar, it was like an epiphany, man. Sometimes I feel like that knowledge holds me back to a certain extent, because if I hadn't figured out real early in life how to be a good street bum, maybe I'd be a mediocre nuclear physicist. I'd be miserable, but I'd be making a whole lot more money.

But honestly, man, I don't really give a fuck about the money. Sure, I need enough to buy food and beer, but that's not the reason I'm out here doing this. I'm out here to be a deprogrammer. Society is composed of people that essentially look like they've been pressed out of a mold. They all shop at the same stores, have the same haircut, the same greedy heartless ideology — totally cultureless, completely uninterested in anything that has any intellectual weight. Work work work, shop shop shop. My music is very essentially antithetical to that. I give people a chance to dig the subversive point of view, to let them

80

Mad Mike the Hippie Bum

know that they don't have to be part of that vicious white trash hellhole of irrational complacency. They have options.

Sure, a lot of people don't always appreciate it. I remember one time I was playing at Thenian's Pub in Jackson, Mississippi. I sang all the hits: "Sex at the Zoo," "Smoking Crack," "I Just Want Your Body," "I Love the Devil." After the show this one guy wrote a letter to the management saying that he was going to burn down the pub if they ever let Mad Mike play there again. I still have that letter. It's probably my most treasured possession. Sometimes, people are so complacent that when that truth hits them it's a hard blow. For people to like it, there's gotta be people that dislike it. I like those people just as much. In fact, I like them even more.

It's a constant struggle, but think about how long it took to end slavery or for women to get the right to vote. It's a hard road. Sometimes I think about what my dad told me when I was thirteen. He said, "If you keep on this path you're going to end up giving blowjobs to dirty old men." That's what he said. But look at me, I'm still on that path and I'm proud to say, that to this day, I haven't given one single blowjob.

Not a one.

81

Russ Ross from Washington D.C.

It happened after Jazz Fest in '95. They had hired me to be a roving minstrel in the artist area and after the festival all the sudden I couldn't hear anything through my left ear. About a month later, the right went out too. I would just sit in my car and try to listen to the radio, but I couldn't even tell what song was on. It was devastating. The doctor said it was a hereditary hearing loss. I'm eighty percent deaf in both ears. There was nothing they could do to fix it.

I got a hearing aide right after that. I could make out conversation, but I still couldn't hear pitch. I couldn't listen to music, I couldn't play guitar. Everything sounded out of tune, like a screeching cat. For ten years, I didn't play music at all. I sold my guitars. For my whole life I was a musician, and then all the sudden it was taken from me.

When Katrina hit, I evacuated to D.C. and I managed to get hooked up with some better insurance. I had to do a lot of wheeling and dealing, but I qualified for this new digital hearing aide. The audiologist made me a custom pair. As soon as I put them in, it was like night and day. I could hear music!

That night, I went to an open mic and borrowed somebody's guitar and got up on stage, and I could actually hear myself sing. It was beautiful. I took my FEMA money and bought myself an acoustic guitar and an amp and started playing again, constantly. I basically had to start all over, getting new calluses on my fingers. It came right back.

When I came back to New Orleans, I was rebuilding houses for a while, working odd jobs here and there. About six months ago, I decided that I was fed up with working for other people, so I started taking my guitar out on the street. That's my only source of income. It's been a real test for my ego, because a lot of people don't know this, but I'm one of the hottest electric guitar players in the world. I was always in bands, jumping around and playing behind my back, playing with my teeth. Out here, I've just got an acoustic guitar and my voice, so I have to be more humble in the way I connect with people.

Now I'm addicted to the street. Everyday's a new adventure. The other night I was out on Royal Street. I looked up and I saw Dr.

John was listening to me. I started playing "When the Wind Cries Mary," and he walked over and started singing with me. My heart was going a mile a minute. Two years ago I couldn't even make out a tune, and now here I am singing with Mac Rebennack. Whoa. It's like I got a whole new lease on life.

Jacob from Chicago

I was waiting for FEMA to send me a string quartet, but I guess I'm playing alone tonight. Wrote this song when I was eighteen years old.

When I split with the old lady, somebody had promised me a job back in Illinois, but when I got there, the job had disappeared, dried up in the Great Illinois Rust Bowl. I ended up working in a mailroom, living in a homeless shelter. I guess the one good thing about living in a shelter is that you don't have to pay rent. I saved up two months worth of paychecks, and then I bought me a brand new acoustic guitar. I ain't a person without my guitar.

Six months later, I lost the job and I almost sold the guitar to get money for cigarettes and rocket fuel. But I got to thinking, instead of sitting there sucking my thumb and feeling sorry for myself, I should go out and play this guitar and see what happens. I got nothing to lose. So I started playing on the streets of Aurora. Police chased me out of there, so I said, you all can go to hell, I'm going to New Orleans.

I got off the Greyhound and didn't know nothing about nothing. You might as well have dropped me in the middle of nowhere and said, now go do it, stay alive. First I started off playing down by the river. Then I worked my way up to Decatur. Ran into a good group of friends who helped me out with a place to stay. No man is a failure that has friends.

My first hurricane was Ivan. I stuck that one out in the Superdome, but they confiscated my wire cutters and all my guitar tools. When Katrina was coming, I said, I'm not gonna do that again, so I ran down to a friend's house in The Marigny. He'd already evacuated, so I had to ride out the whole storm on his porch getting blasted by hundred and fifty mile an hour winds, soaking wet, pieces of roof and two by fours flying all around. I said, God, if you're want me to go, make it quick. If you want me live, get me through this.

Thank God I made it.

Jacob

Sarah Quintana from New Orleans

My grandma's from this huge Cajun family. She's like one of twelve kids or something. They grew up in White Castle, way out on the bayou. She was actually going to become a nun, but then she met my grandfather. He was from an Italian family that ran a cigar shop in the Quarter. Grandma still speaks Cajun, but growing up in the city my dad never learned it. He could catch Grandma when she said a naughty word, but that's about it.

I remember every Carnival season, Grandma used to make these parade parasols, and my parents made me and my sister dance down Canal Street holding them up. For Thoth Parade the whole family would get together in Henry's Bar on Magazine Street, where my mom and dad met each other, and they'd make us do a second line dance on top of the bar. I was really shy and didn't really want to do it. I thought it was dorky.

I started playing guitar when I was fourteen and signed up for a Saturday workshop at NOCCA. I was in Trombone Shorty's class and I sucked really bad. It was a jazz workshop, so it was all these kids with their different instruments and I had this acoustic guitar, so when I soloed, everybody had to go shhh. It was kind of fun, but it really wasn't my level and nobody really wanted to break it down for me.

There's something about jazz where it's kinda like an old men's club. How many times do you see a woman in a brass band? It's like that for a lot of jazz bands too. There's just this stereotype that there's no female jazz guitarists. When the boys made fun of me, I used to go cry with the ballerinas. After I quit NOCCA, I stopped playing jazz for a long time.

Katrina changed everything. My parents' house got totally flooded, so I lost everything. I could deal with that, but the worst part was that for a while I didn't know if my family made it out. It turned out that everybody was OK, but we were spread all over the country.

I travelled for a while, and I really got a sense for how special New Orleans is. Here, I was just another kid with a guitar, but outside I was the Cajun girl from New Orleans. People really respected me for that. Two years ago I got a scholarship to go to France from the

Council for the Development of French in Louisiana. I was supposed to be teaching English, but all the teachers were on strike, so I ended up playing my guitar down by the market in Marseille.

Dixieland Jazz is huge over there, so all those songs I learned back at NOCCA just came back to me. Singing out on the street really taught me how to project my voice. I just felt so comfortable. It's really not that hard. You just have to enjoy yourself. On the street, you just have to give it away for free.

Since I've been back, I've been playing a lot of the French jazz songs that I learned. It's not Cajun music, but my Grandma still loves hearing them. I miss her. She lives with the rest of my family out in Ponchatoula, but I just can't stay away from New Orleans.

Right now I'm only twenty two, so I figure I'm going to give music a shot. There's a lot of people who are helping me right now because they think I have potential to really make it big, but I'm not sure how realistic that is. We'll see how it goes. I'm at the very beginning, for sure.

Editor's Note: Sarah is scheduled to perform at Jazz Fest, 2009.

Sarah and the Soft Shoes performing at The Dragon's Den

Jesse Sewell from New Orleans

First time I started playing guitar for real was 1974. Motorcycle crash — couldn't move anything but my arms. I sat there in bed and I learned how to play Paul Simon's "The Boxer." I could really see myself in that song. I'd just gotten back from the service a few years before, and I was pretty embittered for a long time. If you haven't read John McCain's book about it, he explains it perfectly. I never thought I'd say this, but I didn't get back to feeling patriotic about America until Ronald Reagan became president. It may sound corny but it really was true.

Since '74, I always had a dream of going out and trying to make a living with music, but I had three kids, so their needs trumped that passion for quite some time. When my legs healed up, I ended up working down here at Avondale Shipyard in the labor pen, making minimum wage. From there, I moved up to foreman. I was always pretty good in math, so they sent me to school for design. Pretty soon I ended up helping design ships for Lockheed Shipbuilding.

For twenty years I worked as an engineer. I went from Lockheed Ships to Bell Helicopter to De Havilland Aerospace. When the Columbia went down in 2003, I ended up working for NASA. I was working twelve-hour days on the shuttle, hardly even saw daylight. The money was great, but I was starting to get burned out.

Then along came Katrina. I had two houses on the waterfront south of Slidell — nothing left. The storm really got me thinking about my life. Here I was, sixty-years-old, I was making a bunch of money, but I never really felt satisfied. When I finally beat All State down and got them to pay one hundred percent of the policy, I figured from now on, I was gonna start living on my own terms. For a while I thought about being a shrimper, but then I realized that what I really wanted to do was play my music.

I went back to the wreckage of my house and gathered up some of the storm debris and made this little cart for my amplifiers. The speakers slide in and out like the wings of fighter jet. I've got the tip bucket rigged so that if somebody tries to run off with it, the bottom falls out. I take it out here just about every night.

Jesse Sewell

It's all about living in a capitalist society that allows me to do what I do. Sometimes people stop and listen, sometimes I don't even make gas money. I can't get mad, because nobody asked me to come out here and play. I'm not entitled to anything. I have to earn it. Whenever it gets slow I just close my eyes and I listen to what the guitar sounds like and just get the sweetest, cleanest sound that I can. It's like I'm competing with myself. That's the most honest competition there is.

When I was in the aerospace business, I was uptight and kinda mean spirited. Now I'm nicer than I used to be. It's not because I have to be nice, it's just because nobody can piss me off anymore. I'm like that guy who's driving down the road with his radio blasting singing away. Everybody's looking at him like he's losing it. That's me. I just don't care. I've waited a long time to do this, and I'm not going let anything stop me from having a good time.

Jim lut from Cincinnati

First time I rolled into New Orleans was 1971. I was traveling aournd the country in a van selling hippie jewlery. Back then the sidewalks were a paradise, no T-shirt shops and junk stores to compete with. I set up at the old flea market right next to a snake charmer with a cobra in a basket, and money just came from every direction. It was a real art scene back then, not like the redneck tourists we have now. I used to draw portraits of the tourists, then I started doing oil paintings of Elvis and Mother Theresa. I must have done thousands of portraits. It's good to know that long after I'm gone my art is still gonna be around.

Six or seven years ago, I got burned out on painting, so I just started coming down to the river to play my guitar. I like the solitude. The other street musicians don't fool with me, because nobody wants this spot anyway. The only thing that bugs me is that damn calliope on the steamboat. That thing's so damn loud that you can hear it all the way in Metarie. Sometimes I crank my amp and try to play it down, I never win, but at least I put up a fight.

Since Katrina, I been living in my van. I got a girlfriend who lets me stay with her sometimes. I'm in love with her and it's tearing my heart out that she won't love me the way I want to be loved, but she won't let me loose. It hurts. It hurts real bad.

The only thing that really and truly loves me is this here guitar. Sometimes people stop and listen, sometimes I don't make a dollar all day. Sometimes, it's just one person that makes it worthwhile. The other day I was singing "Old Man River," and this lady just sat down next to me and started crying. She told me that that's the song they were singing over in Algiers when they dropped her off after she was rescued from Katrina. Everybody was soaking wet, lost everything they had, but they were still singing that song.

Times like that are the reason why I'm out here. That's something that I can only get by playing music. Yeah, it's a living, but it's not about the money in the jar.

Jim Iut

Micqual Le Anne from Newport News, Virginia

I like to freestyle. If I'm in a happy mood, I'll sing a happy song. If I'm in a slummed up mood, I sing like it is. It's about having the freedom to share whatever I'm feeling. You see the sign on my case says, "My Music is Free." I mean that. That just doesn't mean that it's free for people to listen to, it means that I'm free when I sing it. I don't make a lot of money, but I always feel appreciated. There's a lot of love out here on these streets.

A year ago, I never would have imagined that I'd be doing this. I was in Virginia with my two kids living in the projects, working two jobs and going to my kids' school everyday trying to be a good mom. One night, my neighbor got in an argument with her boyfriend, and he ended up stabbing her seventy-two times in front of her kids. After that I knew I had to get out of there.

We ended up living in a shelter in Baton Rouge for three months, but that wasn't good for my kids. So from there we came down to New Orleans. Almost as soon as I got here, I found a job and an apartment. I met the love of my life, Óne. He's a street magician and he plays the guitar. He can make that thing talk. I wish he were out here now so you could hear him, but he's home watching my kids and our puppy dog. He's actually giving my little Tequan guitar lessons. Anyways, one night we were at a party and I started to sing along with Óne. He was like, "My God, woman, you can sing. You gotta let the people hear you."

That weekend Óne took me, Tequan and my daughter Nautica out on Royal Street and we sang Christmas carols. It was like the most exotic and explosive feeling just to have people stop and listen to you sing and complement you as an artist. Since then I've been coming out here whenever I can. Yesterday, I even got to sing with Grandpa Elliott.

Tomorrow I'm starting another day job. Don't get me wrong. I love my music, but it don't pay the bills. They call this the Big Easy, but you really have to be on your grind to make sure you don't fall behind. For now, I'm just thankful that I'm blessed enough to share my gift on these streets.

Miqual Le Anne

Lazy Louie from Ohio

I'm stoked. This is the first time I've played this banjo on the street since I rebuilt it. A few weeks ago the head got stuck in the spokes of my bike and snapped right off. It didn't take long to fix, it was just a matter of going to different people's houses to find the tools I needed. The good thing about New Orleans is that when you got a problem, people are always gonna help you out.

I been playing on the street for three years or so. I'd just got out of high school and I was working up at Glacier National Park. This girl told me that she was quitting. I was kind of sweet on her, so I said I'll go with you. We drove out to Seattle and started playing music on the streets. Made thirteen bucks or something. I was like, this is bad ass. What's the point in working when I can just do this?

I rolled into New Orleans like a year and half ago. First night, me and my buddy ended up staying in a house with like ten other people we just met. Fed us beans and taters and everything. I was fartin up a storm, but I was like damn, these are my people — all my long lost friends that I'd never met.

I had this crazy dream last night. I was in a bar or something and these two dudes were doing choreographed dancing — two gay dudes doing this real gay type of dance. I ran right up and joined right in with 'em! It was really weird 'cause I knew all my moves and shit. When I woke up I was like, damn where did that come from? I think maybe it's just saying that a guy can really do whatever he wants in life. Don't matter what people think about you. If I wanted to do a fairy dance, I'd do a fairy dance. If I want to play my banjo, I'll play my banjo. Most people don't realize that. They're scared. I might not have a lot of money, and my banjo might not stay in tune, but at least I ain't scared to do what I want to do in life.

Lazy Louie

Meschiya Lake from Piedmont, South Dakota

The Elk Creek Steakhouse and Lounge, that's the first place I sang in front of an audience. My mother had just left my dad, so she used to go out dancing and take me along and show me how to twostep. I had the time of my life. One night, they announced that they were gonna have a singing contest, so I said, sign me up. I got up there with the Wilkes Brothers Band and sang "Walking After Midnight." I tore the house down. I won five hundred dollars.

My mom loved it. She used to drive me halfway across the state to sing at Star Search competitions. She thought I was gonna be the next Tanya Tucker. Then puberty hit and I started getting into punk rock and skater boys, and I didn't think country music was so hot anymore.

The day after I graduated high school, I jumped on a bus to Chicago to apprentice at a tattoo parlor. I was really miserable there, so I moved to Atlanta and worked a shitty job. I felt like some woman in an old country song, waiting to be rescued. Then one day a traveling circus was rolling through town and their bus broke down. That was my ticket out. I begged them to let me join.

For the next two years I toured with the circus as a clown called Nurse Nasty, spinning fire, eating light bulbs and worms. When we weren't on the road, we wintered in New Orleans.

I'd always been depressed and self-conscious about being an outsider, but in the circus I could take that alienation and turn it into something to be proud of. That's why I got my facial tattoos. I wanted to take that defiance and wear it outwardly. When my mother finally saw them, she cried. I guess she had this image of me as an innocent little girl, and she couldn't imagine anything making that picture more beautiful.

In 2005, I decided to visit some friends at a squat in New York City. That ended up being not such a good thing, because I got strung out on heroin — total self destruction. Then Katrina hit. I was like fuck, my home is gone. I kept thinking about all my friends who might be dead and it shocked me. That night I made up my mind that I was going to detox and go back and help rebuild this city. I knew that

I couldn't do that by being a clown. If New Orleans was going to stay alive it needed music, and I was coming here to sing.

It wasn't easy. It's one thing to shock people eating worms, but to stand on a corner and get people to listen to your music, you really have to be getting true joy out of that moment. I guess for me it's about honesty, getting rid of all my fucked up emotions so I can just be honest about who I really am. That's why I love singing old folk songs and Negro spirituals, the honesty. Those songs were what kept those people going through hard times, and they do the same thing for me.

In the last three years I've sang with a bunch of different bands and even went on tour in Europe with Loose Marbles. I've reconnected with my mother and she's proud of what I'm doing. Now I'm learning how to play my own instruments so that I don't need to rely on a band anymore. Tomorrow, I'm getting on a plane to Germany to tour as a solo performer.

Music saves people. It's saved me. New Orleans is the town that made it happen.

Adrian Thomas from Cincinnati

"Brah, whatcha doing playing that classical music on that violin? That white people stuff? You need to get yourself a saxophone, brah." That's what some guy told me the other day. I just kept playing my Mozart and he just kept walking. A little bit later I was on the same corner and the same guy hit me up for a dollar. I gave it to him. He looked like he needed it.

Before I came to New Orleans, I was working as a network tech for a Fortune 500 corporation. There were two hostile takeovers, and you're living on borrowed time all the time. It gave me nightmares. By 1993, I was unemployed, so I came down to New Orleans to ship out as a merchant seaman. I was having a problem with the paperwork, and so I just started playing music on the streets. One night, I was on Royal and Toulouse and this guy came by in his truck and he yells out the window, "Hey man, can you play Cajun music?"

I said, "I can play anything." I'd never played Cajun music in my life. Next thing you know I'm playing in a Cajun band on Bourbon. A year later, I was touring with a ballet about the Acadian Exile. We did four shows at Lincoln Center and then we went to Europe — sold out shows. Actually Helsinki wasn't sold out, but there was a Cajun band from north Finland that came and they tried to cook for us. The rest of the band wouldn't eat it, because they put reindeer meat and zucchini in the jambalaya, but I thought it was great. You never know where the streets are gonna take you.

Tanya Huang from Taiwan

It's a lot like surfing. Most of the time you're just paddling out. I'm lucky if in three hours I get ten seconds of a wave, but it's worth it. Everything just clicks and your mind, body and spirit becomes one and the music just flows without really having to think about it. It happens very rarely, but that's what I live for, passion — the feeling of fulfillment and peace.

Sometimes people will stop by and listen and say, oh that's really great, you should be in a symphony. At one point I actually did play in a symphony. Some people love it, but for me that was so boring. You dress up exactly like they tell you. You play exactly how they tell you. You're like a robot. When I'm out here, I'm creating and improvising, reinventing myself at every moment. It's like the complete opposite. I'll take the street over the symphony any day.

I moved to New Orleans five years ago. My friend Dorise plays guitar and she persuaded me to come down and play with her on the streets. We were broke all the time. I kept telling Dorise that I needed to find a job as a waitress, but she was like, don't get a job, we can do this. It was really hard. What made it OK was having friends to

Dorise Blackmon, guitar virtuoso

help us out.

Before Katrina we used to play inside clubs more. These days the clubs can't really afford to pay musicians, so now we do better on the street. Dorise and I were actually some of the first street musicians to come back after the storm, playing for the Red Cross and the National Guard. It was weird not seeing the tourists and little kids, but we thought that it was more important than ever to come out here and play, not just to entertain, but to be able to reach out to people.

I really feel like the future's unwritten. I've always been such a free spirit, my life has been totally random so far. I remain open. In twenty years I might still be on the street, or in a coffee house, or a giant stage, but if I'm not doing what I enjoy, it doesn't matter. For now, I'm just honored to be able to play on these streets for the people of New Orleans.

Editor's Note: Dorise Blackmon's story will be featured in the second edition.

Alexander Masakela from New York City

My horn is nothing more than a gambit to get your attention. Like, you recall when the king is coming they blast the trumpet, dant dah da dah, then the king can give his speech. That's how I get your attention. Hello! I'm over here. Sit down and talk with me. I love people. I get life from people. I do. Like when you stand in the rain on a hot day you feel that water hitting you and it cools you off. It's the same for the spirit. If my spirit be hot and bothered, I talk to people, and that cool soothing humanity of mankind mists over me, I feel so relaxed and calm. Didn't always used to be like that. There were times in my life when I hated people. Now, people are what I live for.

A lot of the people I see walking around in the French Quarter, they're drowning. They don't know how to swim in the world. They're out there in that raging river and they're flapping their arms. I'm gonna get my clothes wet and jump in that nasty river and I'm gonna show you my format. Just relax. Lay on your back, breathe. Hold on. See music is my backstroke. If you let that backstroke get you outta that deep water, you're gonna make it to the beach. Then we're gonna sit down on the banks and have a talk. What you doing in that water over there? Lets talk about that.

Do I make sense? A lot of people say I talk crazy, they can't follow me at all. I think it's because they're too worried about details. It's like, you're looking at a painting, and all you can see is one brush stroke. Your brain doesn't have enough information to make a picture. You can't see all the different colors, because you're too focused on one color, the color of the now. But the now doesn't exist. Touch my hand. See? It's in the past already. It only exists in your memory. But what is wisdom? Memory. Our thinking process is no more than the fruit of our past. I'm a blessed man because I remember everything that has ever happened to me.

Editor's Note: To read Alexander's life story visit sidewalksaints.com

Doc Lewis from Atlanta

What you wanna hear? Blues? Jazz? Dixieland? Gospel? Do you have a camera? A camera phone? OK, stand right here. Let me see your hand. You're not just gonna hear the music, you're gonna feel the music. This is gonna be the best picture of your whole vacation.

My daddy was the first black police officer in Atlanta, Georgia. He was proud to be a cop, even through he couldn't arrest a white man. The only thing he could do was hold you until a white cop come. That's how bad it was in the South. It was shitty man. I remember when they had the school boycott, my daddy sent me to school anyways. Only four students showed. My daddy had to be a sucker ass, because he was scared. Everybody was trying to find out shit on my daddy to knock him outta the picture. I was under the microscope too. It was like living on pins and needles. School, I always had straight A's from first grade all the way up. I was smart, man. It's nothing you can ask me that I can't answer.

First time I picked up a trombone was summer going into tenth grade. The band director, he let me take one home for the summer. When I got back that September, I was a better musician than my band director. I even told him he was teaching music wrong. Boy, my band director was jealous. Coming out of school, he was giving everybody scholarships to Bethune Cookman, but he didn't give me one.

I got drafted by the Army, so I ran real quick and took the Air Force test. I was trying to get myself in the Special Services so I could be in the Air Force Band and avoid Vietnam, but the recruiters fucked me up. I ended up being air police. Went to Vietnam and got shot twice. I did four years. I was happy to get out. I burned my uniform at the gate when I left, put kerosene on it and tossed it out the window.

Coming out of the service, I hooked up with Archie Bell. He was down in Houston, Texas, and he put me in the musicians union. I met a singer by the name of Lynn Collins, they call her Mamma Feel Good, and she told James Brown about me. James was out in California and he needed a horn player, so he bought me a ticket out there. Fred Wesley gave me a little audition to see what I could do.

Man, I showed Fred up. Damn, we sounded good.

Playing with Brown was like being in the service. You got a scuff mark on your shoe, a wrinkle on your uniform, you miss a note on stage, he'll fine you a hundred dollars. If Brown didn't think your stuff was tight, he'd send somebody to the hotel to make sure you were practicing in your room. I'm gonna be honest with you, it wasn't thrilling to work for James Brown. That man was hard. Three times I quit that man's band. The turnover ratio was high with Brown.

One day we were rehearsing, and he didn't like something about the way I was playing and he called me "boy." I got up and cursed him out real beautiful in front of the whole band. I told him, "If you ever get your legs around your neck, you'd have room to get your head out your ass!"

It felt good, damn good. I wish I could do that every day. I didn't need James Brown. I let him know that. But that's when he started respecting me. As I was walking away he started to say, "Come mere boy, uh mister, uh doc, Doc Lewis! Come here, you gonna be Doc from now on." I kept walking. He called me at the hotel and asked me how much money I want to stay in the band.

I told him, "Mr. Brown, it's not about the money, it's about respect." I didn't do what I did for me, I did it for the whole band. "You gotta start respecting your band."

He said, "I'll tell you what, I'm still gonna do my thing, but I will adhede to that." That's what he said, "adhede." Sometimes he just mumbled and jumbled his words. And wouldn't you know it, he gave me a hundred thousand dollars to stay in the band.

I stayed with Brown until he went to jail in 1988. You know the real reason he went to jail? He went into the middle of a meeting of the KKK with a shotgun. They called the cops on him and that's when the chase started. They got him for drunk driving, but the real charge was assaulting people with a shotgun. I was with him. I know.

I moved down to New Orleans, because I wanted to see all this good food, music, and women. I thought I would be on stage, but I fell in love with the street. See, what I do on the corner is a show. Letting the tourists take pictures with their hand on my horn, I'm the only one that does that. See, I got to be original. I don't come out here to play. This is just something I do 'cause I like to have fun with the people. To me it's like a vacation. Out here, I spend more time talking than I do playing.

When I'm not out here, I'm still playing my ass off. I got me a little suitcase packed up so I can get right to the airport when somebody needs me to fly to a gig. Right now, I'm playing with Gladys Knight. I'm also putting together my own band and it's gonna be the best in the world. It's gonna be funky man. You'll see.

Hell, you ain't even seen me play for real yet. I'll challenge anybody, walk right up on 'em without rehearsing. I'm cocky man. I can't help that part. Watch this, you hear that band on Bourbon? I'm gonna walk in there and take that shit over right now.

Y'all got any James Brown?

Doc stepping in with the band at The Famous Door

David and Roselyn
from Riverside, California and Flint, Michigan

David: Basically, we're like farmers. After the big harvest farmers sell the wheat, but all through the year they're selling the eggs. It's the same thing for us. When we go on tour that's our wheat, but when we come out on the street that's our eggs. On Royal Street you get it fresh from the chicken. Lots of great blues, jazz, folk and whatever we feel like.

Roselyn: We've been coming out here since 1974. Back then we were touring around the country in a big old school bus. It was cut in half with a set of dutch doors in the middle and the rest was open. We'd be going down the highway and the kids and I would grab the posts and swing around. People going down the road would be like, "Oh no!"

David: Dumb Hippies.

Roselyn: Dare devils not hippies. I hate being called a hippie. I am a dare devil and a radical and so are my kids. We were leaving New Orleans and our transmission went bloop. The bus went back into the shop and we looked for gigs. Feeling sad, I took my guitar to Jackson Square, sat on the grass, closed my eyes and started playing the blues. When I opened my eyes about a half hour later, there was seven bucks in my case. Whooeee! We eat tonight! So we started being street musicians.

David: For the first few years we were in and out of New Orleans, but then when the kids got to the age where they wanted to be in school, we decided to move down here. Al Jaffe from Preservation Hall let us live in our van on his vacant lot in the Treme. Eventually we moved into an apartment. Now we have our own house in the Bywater. We're pretty much middle class.

Roselyn: David's middle class. I'm upper class.

David and Roselyn

Wilsoni the Balloonatik from The Bronx

When I was first learning how to perform in front of an audience, I used to do what they call productions of live animals, magically producing a white dove from a handkerchief. You don't hear many magicians talk about this, but you have to load everything beforehand. I was doing a show for a radio station in Chicago, and they had me in the green room and I was waiting to go on. My heart's racing and I'm ready to go out there and the guy comes in and says, five more minutes. OK, so I took a deep breath and calmed down. Five minutes later, he comes back in and says another five minutes. A half hour later he says, OK you're on. So, I go out there on stage. I'm dressed well. I'm speaking well. Everything is going great. I went to produce my dove and he doesn't flap his wings.

He had passed on.

My immediate reaction was that my best friend had died, because he was. We had practiced and practiced. But then my next thought was, I'm on stage, what do I do? I started flapping his wings with my fingers to make it look like he was still alive, then I pushed him away. The audience never knew.

I flubbed it up. Every time you flub up it teaches you something, but that was the hardest lesson to learn. Always be aware of your time. Time is critical. I also learned that shit is gonna happen, and you have to try to come out with your head on top.

My family was Jehovah Witness, and in some ways they tend to be very fanatical about their beliefs. You were never allowed to question anything, and I just had a lot of doubts that were never answered. I was always a rationalist, I thought things should make sense. I loved math and science, because it was something I could put my finger on. I remember one afternoon our science teacher took us to the filming of a TV show and they showed us different science projects on stage. In one part of the program they had a magician take a woman from the audience and levitate her. I'm like, wow, he was like a god, but I knew that there had to be a rational explanation for what he was doing. The magician was just keeping it a secret. I figured maybe if I could learn those secrets, then maybe I could be a god too.

Eventually I started going to a magic store and buying some tricks. I met some other magicians, but magic is like its own little society. It's a protected type of art where you don't tell secrets to just anybody. Once they saw that I had the stamina and the intellect to be true to the art, some of them took me under their wing and showed me some things. I was a nerdy kid, a bookworm, very introverted. Magic was something that really helped bring me out of my shell.

Magic was always something that I did on the side. I never really thought it could pay the bills. After high school I got married and had a kid, so I went to college and got a degree in electronics. We moved out to Chicago, and when I went to an employment agency, they were so impressed with me that they offered me a job working for them. After a while it started bothering me, because sometimes I would be on the phone with employers and they'd tell me that they didn't want to hire any black people. They didn't know I was black. It was very disturbing, but I had to feed my family.

It all came down when I lost my daughter. She was five-years-old. That hit me hard. I lost the world. It's still hard to think about it. I was blaming everything and everyone. I started drinking real heavily and my marriage fell apart. I quit my job and just left town for a while.

I happened to be passing through New Orleans and I saw a magician on the street. He wasn't that good, but he was making goo gobs of money. I said this is the life. It just kind of struck me like a wand. Most people remember their first love, their first kiss, and I still remember my first street show. I think I only made about fourteen dollars, but I knew immediately that I wasn't going back to Chicago. Magic saved me, because I wasn't sitting there feeling sorry for myself. I was constantly working on my act.

The streets are a great place to learn. When you're performing on a stage, you can follow a set routine, but as a street performer you have to constantly adapt your show according to your audience. Probably the most important thing that I've learned over the past twenty years is that you have to develop your own style. My attitude is that I'm the best. I'm not saying I'm the best magician out there, but I'm the best at doing my show. I've had magicians come up to me and say, I could do your act. David Blaine told me that in Washington Square in New York. I'm not sure if he could. He might be able to do the tricks that I do, but as far as getting a large crowd involved, getting them comfortable and having them pay you, he wouldn't be able to do that the exact same way I do. That's something that you can't mimic. Nobody can do my show but me.

There are two shows that I've done in New Orleans that really stick out in my mind. One time this guy laid down on his back right in front of the audience. I thought, oh man, another drunk who's gonna wreck my show. Then he took out his checkbook and wrote me a five hundred dollar check. He says, "I don't care about these other people, just perform for me." So I did my whole show in front of this guy, he gave me the check and it actually cleared — only in New Orleans. Another time I was passing the hat, and there was a guy watching from a balcony. He was a little inebriated and he took a quarter and flung it at me. It hit me dead center in the forehead, blood is dripping down my face. The audience is like, oh my god this is real. The guy started to run, but some people in the audience chased him down and brought him back to me. The cops asked me if I wanted him arrested. I said, no. It's not nice to have to spend New Year's Eve in jail.

When I first started performing, I was basically just concerned

about survival, making the rent and groceries. I had a lot of friends who made it big in entertainment, and it went to their head. I pretty much figured that would happen to me too, so I never really made much effort to promote myself. Then, after the birth of my third child, I realized that I had to get more serious about the business aspect. I still haven't made any real breakthroughs, but I'm still staying focused. I'm still not satisfied, but I can't complain. I've definitely found my niche here in New Orleans and I know that only better things can come.

Oh yeah, you can catch me next week on the Jay Leno Show — I'll be in the third row from the back.

Alexander the Magician from Ann Arbor

Magic just sort of happened. I got the magic kit for Christmas when I was five-years-old with the cups and balls. For years that's all I practiced. Cups and balls embodies just about every magic technique out there, slight of hand, palming, misdirection. It's totally pure because there are no gimmicks, no boxes that fold apart and do the trick for you. It's just your hands and the balls. Balls are huge. If you're performing on the street, my god, you need a set of balls.

I did my first professional show at a nursing home. Unless you're performing show tunes, a nursing home is probably the roughest crowd ever. I was a close up trick kid, but they were all lined up against the wall. So I started on one end and worked my way across. "Mam, pick a card."

"Oh she's asleep."

"Mam pick a card."

"Oh she's blind."

I was so terrible I didn't even ask them to pay me. If there's such thing as a miracle, it's a miracle that I'm still performing after that. But I'd have to say that it's good to fall on your ass at least the first hundred times. The more shots you miss, the more you'll make.

All through college I did corporate shows: business meetings, luncheons, restaurants. One time they even flew me out to Chicago to work a fragrance company convention. In the corporate world people know they came to see a show, so you don't have to work as hard to get the audience behind you. It was great for my confidence, but after a while my routine started to become robotic. It was like I was a dancing monkey.

When I got to my last semester of college, I was totally disgusted with the direction my magic was taking. I was spending more time on the phone trying to line up gigs than I was working on my technique. Then I started going on youtube and watching all these street magicians. Their command was just electric. It was the opposite of what I was doing. They did what they wanted, when they wanted, and they made as much as they were worth. I was like, damn, I need this challenge. I got a van with a little mattress in the back and took off

to take on the streets.

All along the East Coast I tried to do what I thought of as a street show, but I couldn't get a crowd to stop. It was terrible. I'd just left a very lucrative world, but on the streets I couldn't do shit. I hardly made a dollar until I got to New Orleans.

I had a lot of help from other magicians, Doug Conn, Jimmy Talksalot. I probably learned the most from Warpo. He taught me that it really doesn't matter how good your skills are, if you can't connect with the crowd. The show isn't about the tricks, it's about you. You are the show. Warpo and I traded spots for a while, and he helped me out with my routine. By the end of the week, I had a day where I made sixty bucks. I was like yes! I'll never have to work again.

I love the crowds here in New Orleans, because they're such a mishmash. One minute I could be performing for Christian missionaries and then the next, it's crack addict street kids. The people here are less inhibited, so you can always get volunteers, but they're also not afraid to call you out. The other day I was doing this trick with a handkerchief and a coin, and this little girl was standing right at my feet. She looks up and says to the whole crowd, "There's a big coin under there." Destroyed the climax, but the audience loved it.

Right now, I'm living in an RV over on the West Bank. I'm still not making as much money as I used to, but I'm definitely much happier than when I was doing the corporate stuff. When I have a good show, I feel like I've earned it. To stop a complete stranger on the street and have them walk away with a sense of wonder, if I can make that happen, I feel like I can make anything happen.

That's magic.

Johnny Balloons from New York City

Feel my hands, how soft they are. They're like baby's hands. I can tie a knot in anything. I could have been a surgeon, but I don't like blood. You know I'm sixty-years-old now, and I'm just as quick as the boxer I was when I was sixteen. Just as quick — and just as deadly. Hah! You wanna arm wrestle?

I grew up in a magic shop. Tannens, greatest magic shop in the world. By age thirteen I was one of the best slight of hands you'll ever see. Used to run the three card monte in Times Square. Took a little break when I went in the service. When I got out, I was back running the road hustling. I didn't have a clue what was going on in my life, thirteen years I wasted. In October of 1982, I didn't wanna spend the winter in New York, so I got on a bus to New Orleans to come down here and do street magic.

At the time two of the greatest magicians in the world were here, Cellini and Rocky. I couldn't compete. I was in trouble. I ran into one of the best balloon guys at that time, Ron Dunagon. He had no place to stay, so I let him share my room and he taught me balloons.

For twenty-six years that's what I been doing. If I feel like going to work, I go to work. If I feel like sleeping, I sleep. I don't eat at five star restaurants, but I can make you a homade tomato sauce you'd die for. It would make the Italian mammas in New York on Ninth Avenue shake.

Hey you dropped your socks!
Gottcha.

Johnny Balloons

Page1ne from New Orleans

As far as keeping my focus, I learned that from a bet. When I was a kid, my friends would say, I bet you can't flip off the house for a Snicker or a pack of cookies. I used to put my shoes down not even realizing I was going head forward. I wasn't really thinking about controlling my body, I just flipped. I just basically kept doing it, not being scared to fall. I'm self taught. Everything you see me do, it came from me.

I'm from the Ninth Ward. Grew up around killers and pimps and drug dealers and all that. My own pa, I guess I'm gonna say sperm donor, was a pimp. That's what he did, had women, ho's on the corner. But by me entertaining and flipping, I got lucky enough not to have be in that circle. And you know what? Those drug dealers and killers still respect us to this day. They say, you guys are great and my children love you, but they done killed ten people. See, those guys got respect, but it's a respect that comes from fear. We got a different kind of respect where we don't have to be looking over our shoulders. The police stop me on the corner, they're gonna be looking for pictures and autographs. You see my picture in the paper, I'm gonna be smiling.

When we started off, we used to dance on cardboard boxes underneath the I-10. The sweat would start breaking up the box and then you'd be down on the concrete getting war wounds. We saw moves on TV, but we didn't know it was called breaking or flooring or b-boying. We just saw an opportunity to do our own thing. My cousins were into it too, so we just decided that we was gonna form our own little group, The Dragon Master Showcase. By us being related, we have that communication. If there's a problem we can tell each other without having to worry about seeming like we're downing somebody. We got to have each other's back, because if one of us gets hurt, the other guy's gonna step it up.

1983, we started taking it out to the streets in the French Quarter. At first we were just doing straight moves, but pretty soon we realized you get a better crowd if you joke around and make the tourists a part of it. You see, anybody can do dance moves, but not everybody can do a dance show. Nobody leaves here saying that was a

great flip, or that was a great spin, they say that was a great show.

We've taken shit for the racial humor plenty of times, but what we're doing is actually bringing people together. I don't care if you're black, white, Puerto Rican or Asian. We're gonna go there. Like when we're collecting tips, we might say, "It keeps us outta the poor house — and outta your house." See, we say something in a show and it's funny, but people really think that way. Like one time this white guy seen me walking down the street and he locked up his car doors — and he's in a convertible. I got no choice but to laugh at that shit. By making people laugh, what we're really doing is giving them a chance to think about how stupid those attitudes are. You see, out here we got the United Nations, all types of people, and everybody's just having a good time. We probably performed for the Grand Wizard of the KKK, but he's out here sitting next to a black person and he laughing. He might go back to being ignorant after that, but for one hour he forgot about that.

When we started performing, it was fun. Then we started making money and it got real fun. When we started traveling, it got even more fun. Now I love America, but in Europe it seems like people appreciated it three hundred percent more. It's great to be able to go to different places, because you learn so much. Like when we went to South Africa to perform for Nelson Mandela's birthday, I saw people living in cardboard boxes, no food, no water, but they proud, they didn't pity themselves. After the show I gave this guy like twenty dollars and he was crying. I said what's the matter? He said he was happy because his family could eat for a month. Twenty dollars for a month!

I feel really lucky that God has blessed me with the opportunity to do something that I wake up in the morning and I love doing. We make it look easy, because we're having fun. I tell anybody, you know what the Fountain of Youth is? Being physical and having fun. Nobody know our ages, we look like kids. That's the secret.

Editor's Note: Page and his cousin Lil Countrie placed second in the nation on America's Got Talent in 2008.

Deatrick Holley "Goldie" from Memphis

Now here comes Goldilocks with Old Big Shoulders. Bad Boy you know you did good! Got the pretty baby. Made your mamma proud!

Yeah baby! It's Goldie! How you doing baby? Boo ya ya! All right now! Wear them jeans girl.

That's a bad dude, I thought that that one boy had two a them pretty women. All right, Dad! Laissez les bons temps rouler!

This here is the French Quarters. We outlaws down here, son and I'm undefeated. Back up boys, y'all get your cameras ready, looks like it's fixed be a shooting. Stand back, we about to slap some leather. One. Two. Three. BAM! Another one bites the dust! This here is Goldie the Bourbon Street Cowboy, fastest gun in the French Quarters. That's how old boy here makes a living, putting 'em on boot hill. Won't you all do the sweet thing and bless the box for me? Thank you, Dad. You all are so lovely. I hope that you and these fine young ladies have a wonderful evening.

Deatrick Holley "Goldie"

What the tourists want is to be validated, to know that they're having a good time and that their presence is appreciated. This here is Goldie baby! Twenty-four karats! I come to life and give 'em a real show. I dance, I sing, I strut and sway with an animal grace. Let 'em know this is the Big Boy's Playground, and ain't nobody ringing the bell, cause we're at recess forever.

I came down to New Orleans in '96. I'd been working at Amtrak in Memphis, and they said they had a promotion for me down here. I come into town all suited and booted, and then when I show up at the station, they say that they had to give the job to some other guy. OK, that left me high and dry in New Orleans, highly pissed off. I'm walking around here and I'm down to seventeen hundred dollars. Oh Lord, what to do? I looked at these boys with the silver standing on the crates, and I said I can do that, but I'm gonna be totally different. I'm gonna be gold.

I called up a laboratory in Hollywood and told 'em I needed makeup that I could wear without turning into a greasy gobbly mess. I can't tell you the secret formula, because I don't want these other boys out here to catch on, but this here is twenty-four karat. Solid gold baby! My makeup is meticulous. My mustache stays looking like

Clark Gable, and that's what you want. You want that accentuated look. I'm gorgeous! Not a one can come and be as handsome in their presentation — tall, gold and brutally handsome.

I started out on Decatur Street. That's where you got Granny and Grandpa, Auntie and Uncle, all the kids and everything. Yeah, they tip, but they want a hundred photos for a single dollar. That's too slow for me. That's what I now call the Disney Channel. So I got up in my saddle and went out to ride that horse called Bourbon Street. I still ride him better than anybody down there. I'm the King of Bourbon Street.

I got fans that come back year after year. The sweeties they understand that's how I make my living, so the ones that come back annually usually tip me a hundred dollars. That's cool. I got others who don't work for Microsoft or something, they pay me twenties, tens. I love 'em. One particular judge over in Baton Rouge keeps a big picture of him and Goldie right there in his office. That's a big compliment. It is. I'm thrilled internally by it.

A couple years ago, they actually tried to stop street performers in the Quarter. There was this one particular councilwoman, I can say her name, because she's already mad at me: Jackie Clarkson. But I ain't mad at her. I have no axe to grind. Now Miss Clarkson's background is in real estate, and she had aspirations of turning the French Quarter in condominiums and getting rid of all the street entertainment. They had a sixteen-man task force. They came out here and arrested me in the middle of my show, took me to jail and charged me with obstructing a public passage. They figured if they knocked off Goldie, all the other entertainers would get the message. It really hurt me that she would do that, but when I got to court and I stood before the judge, he looked at me and said, "I know you. You're Goldie. You do a mighty fine show."

I said, "Thank you your honor."

Then he said, "As a matter of fact my wife and I, we took a picture with you."

"You did your honor?"

"We sure did."

"Did you tip me?"

The judge started laughing. "Yes, I did Goldie, five dollars."

"Boo ya ya!"

The whole court started cracking up. The judge ordered me

released immediately, then he told the prosecutor not to fill up his court with this frivolity. Since then, I haven't had any problems with the city. As a matter of fact, after Katrina, Ray Nagin showed up at the town meeting in Memphis and said, "Goldie come home. We need you." Mayor Nagin told me, "Goldie, my door is always open to you." I'll always respect him for that. Since Katrina, I think the city is starting to realize that the street performers are one of the main reasons that tourists come to New Orleans. It's unique. This is the only city in America where something like this is possible. A character like Goldie, put him in Boston, they'd be calling the SWAT team on him.

Tonight, I'll probably work two or three hours. That's the nice thing about working for the I Say So Corporation. Whatever I say so, that's what I do. The crowd can tell if you really got the juice flowing, so if Goldie's not ready, I don't try to bring him out. There's no faking out here. If it don't come from the star that's in you, then it ain't gonna shine. It's gotta be twenty-four karats.

For the first couple years, I just went at it full throttle all day long, but as the years have gone by it's starting to tax me so much physically. With my diabetes, there are some boundaries that I have to respect. Some nights I have to stay home and just be Deatrick Holley

— tall, *dark* and brutally handsome.

Alright handsome! You did good, got the pretty baby! Made your mamma proud!

You see that? They smile, walk away, grab each other's hand and share a special moment. When they go back to working in the office or driving the forklift in the warehouse, they're gonna remember that moment, and pretty soon they'll be coming back to the French Quarters. I'm telling you, Goldie's a part of what's gonna bring New Orleans back.

Deatrick Holley "Goldie"

Tim the Gold Guy from various US Army Bases

I got drunk. All this happened cause I got drunk on Bourbon Street. It was fourteen years ago, man. I was driving cross the country in my Delta '88. Got stuck out in the bayou, and the car ran out of gas. It ain't had no battery left in the battery, so I just left the car behind and went to the Brantley Center. I didn't have no choice. It's a homeless shelter. It's a scary situation, bro, actually it was. You don't even know where you're going or what you're gonna do. So, I sold hotdogs for a long time. Learned how to juggle the mustard and the catsup like Tom Cruise in Cocktail. That's good for a five or ten dollar tip every once in a while. I made my money, but it took up too much of my life.

I remember all of it. This is how I started. One night, I got drunk, bro, on Bourbon Street. I saw a silver guy and he was standing still. I said, well I don't have no money, so I put my empty beer glass in the middle of Bourbon Street and I stood up on one foot and I pointed to the glass. Like this. I'll show you the pose. Just like this. I've got good balance, I'm the best, bro. Ten minutes, that bitch was fulla money. The silver dude got mad and run me off. He got really pissed.

I said, hmm, if I could do that like that, I wonder what I could do in a day standing on a crate. I don't remember half of how I actually come up with all the rest of it 'cause I was drunk. Like the sweatshirt. I don't ever remember how I come up with the sweatshirt. Then I threw the crate aside and I said, I'm gonna do something that nobody's ever done before. To hell with the crate, I'm just gonna do it on my feet. Somehow, I come up with The Pose. I was drunk when I come up with that one too. Nobody can do The Pose. Nobody. I'm double jointed, bro. I'm the only one in the country that does this that's double jointed. That makes me the best in the country already. I take em down, dude. You seen it with your own eyes.

Hell yeah, I quit selling hotdogs after that. Who wants to sit there for twelve thirteen hours a day. I could sit there right here for five minutes standing still bro, and I ain't got no boss, no nobody — but the police is my boss. I went to jail twenty six times doing this. Obstruction of the sidewalk. But now that I been on TV and shit, they're like, what do you gotta fuck with the Gold Guy for? Everybody

knows me in this town.

I'm on front covers of magazines. So far this year I made the front cover of *Where Y'at* with Tyson Chandler from The New Orleans Hornets. I'm on a Morris Bart commercial. I won third place in the Stella Contest.* I got drunk and I mimed it. If you come to my house, I'll show you my trophies. I got a Wall of Tim and what it is is it's a bunch of things that I've accomplished. See that ball rolling, that's me. Just trust me. You're gonna see me. I got a new commercial coming out for the New Orleans Saints. Wait 'til you see it.

Man, this is kinda crazy, dude. The craziest thing about everything is that I can't pick up a woman dressed like I normally dress up, but when I dress up in gold, I pick up all the women I want to in the whole fucking world. Ain't that something? You dress up in gold, ah shit, you can get laid any time you want. Yeah. You dress up in gold, it'll work. It does every time — every ex-wife I have.

It's kinda crazy though how life treats you. I seen so many people die, so many people that I know who've passed away, because they made the wrong decisions, got their ass beat or got murdered. That's the only thing that really bothers me. You know, it really does bother me every time I lose somebody. My fiancé just passed away. I told her about the streets. I told her how it is and things like that and she didn't listen. Now she's dead.

She came in from out of town, I took her off the street, gave her a place to live in my house, got her a job as a waitress. Then the hurricane took us away for a little bit. And she fucked up. She fucked up real bad. You know, she was a stripper man, she was evil. Yeah she's evil bro, and I lost her. Yeah, and she got her shit from the same place where she worked at. She got the shit. I said, I don't do that shit. She took one line of that shit and it killed her. Straight up killed her.

Yeah, so man, you think you've got battles, dude, you ain't seen nothing. I cry every night. I cry every night. Yeah, I loved that lady, she was fine. And she had some good ass, you know. Now she's gone. Dude, you just don't even know.

Tomorrow, I'm going to the Superdome, gonna play for the Saints. They got me doing The Pose in the parking lot. Gave me free tickets and everything, you can come along, I'll get you into the game. But Tuesday, I'm heading out to Pascagoula, Mississippi. Got me a

*Contest to reenact Marlon Brando's shout in *Street Car Named Desire*

friend who got hit real bad by the hurricane. Their financial situation is kind of rough. I'm gonna help 'em build a house. That's what I used to do before I became the Gold Guy, before I came to New Orleans. I was just Tim the House Builder. The money ain't a thing. I'm gonna go over there and pitch a tent and help them out. Then I'm gonna sit there by the catfish pond, gonna do my yoga, then I'm gonna throw my line in the catfish pond, and I'm gonna think about shit for a while.

Larry the Leprechaun from various USAF bases

First time I came to New Orleans I was fifteen-years-old, ran away from home. I got dressed up in my band uniform, picked up my trombone and just started hitchhiking. I looked so young, every ride, I'd tell them that I just missed the band bus and all they had to do was get me up the road so I could catch up with the rest of the band. When I got here, I played my trombone on street corners. If I could get together the money for a room, I slept there. If not, I'd sleep under a tree. Nobody ever bothered me. It was a great time.

This was during Vietnam, and all the service men were walking around in uniforms. One night, I'm playing for a bunch of sailors dressed up in their whites. They offered me twenty dollars to play at a party. It turned out to be a hotel room with two twin beds and about twenty-five sailors lined up for two whores. I'm fifteen years old, very much a virgin, and not feeling so comfortable in there, so after about ten minutes, I was out the door. I have no idea where I am. All the sudden, a police car squeals on the brakes and the officer rolls down the window, "What the fuck are you doing here, honky?" I was walking right though the middle of the projects.

My mother had to come and get me all the way from Panama City, and then I ended up going to reform school. Through that I picked up a lot of bad habits, so I ended up in reform school again. By the time I turned eighteen, I was a little hippie and I'd had it with my family, so I dropped out of high school and took off. I don't really wanna say what I was involved in, but it entailed me running between Atlanta and the West Coast pretty regularly. I was always stopping over in New Orleans for longer and longer, and then I realized I fucking love this town. Why couldn't you?

Jimmy Dixon, he was one of the top magicians in the South. He and I got to talking, and he hired me to be his helper. Jimmy had this shtick where he used to block off a whole street, and he'd be put in a straight jacket with chains wrapped around him. In the meantime, he's got carpenters building a crate around him. At the other end of the block, a drag racer with a cow catcher on the front was revving its engine, vroom vroom. He'd start a big clock that would count down

for sixty seconds while he'd try to get out of the crate. You'd see the crate shaking and moving, then the car would take off and smash right through BAM! Splinters everywhere. Everyone's going, "Oh no! That bugger's still in there." Then Jimmy would magically step out from behind the crowd. Now, of course, the straight jacket was a gimmick, the chains were a gimmick, but the biggest gimmick of all was that they built the crate over a manhole. He'd go straight down through the sewer for a block and then pop right back up.

I worked with Jimmy for a few years, but carnival life is rough, so I started thinking about something where I could just work the Quarter. I came up with this concept called the Gorilla Man. I swear its original with me. It's a six foot gorilla that carries a cage in front of him with a guy in it. My upper body in the cage is real, but my legs were really the gorilla's legs. I had a little coconut for a tip bucket.

People would see me walking down the street and they'd just about drop their drinks. I'd have bananas, and I'd try to bribe the gorilla to put me down. Where I really made my money was going into the clubs and dancing. The band would start playing and the gorilla would start tapping his foot, and then I'd say, "Oh no, you can't do this, put me down, don't start dancing, please!" Gads, I could spin that cage. But never as drunk as I got, and I would get drunk, did I ever fall down in front of a band. The bar owners loved it, because I was bringing in crowds of forty, fifty people. The money was amazing, but the the costume was so heavy, I could only work three hours a day.

One day, my landlord's half wit caretaker came across the costume in the shed and decided that it was trash and threw it out. By that time, I was so tired of dragging that thing around that I was like, oh, thank you, time to move on to something else. You've gotta understand, I'm constantly reinventing myself. I've never been stuck in a rut. Never.

In 1992, my mother bought me a camcorder and I started going out on Bourbon Street and making movies of the girls flashing their tits from the balconies. For twelve years that's how I supported myself, selling those videos on the Internet. I had a pretty good run until Girls Gone Wild started running infomercials. Not only was there no competing against them, they made the girls scared of being on television. By the time Katrina hit, I was pretty much belly up.

I had a friend, everyone called him John the Pervert, we were talking last December, and we came up with the idea for the leprechaun. When I first came out, I was a dwarf leprechaun. I had a little platform with holes for my feet, and then I cut the soles out of a pair of size fourteen shoes so they fit around my knees. I did that for one day and the wood was rubbing all over my knees, hurt like a bastard. OK, so no dwarf, which was OK, because now I realize that it's all about the movement. The more I move the more attention I get. I love working stop signs, making it look like I'm trying to hide behind them. It's so ludicrous, people start laughing, then they're gonna want a picture, and I'm gonna get a tip. It's all energy, all energy. Soon as you can put a smile on their faces, you're gonna make a living.

Right now, I'm fifty-nine years old. I've seen this scene when it first started blossoming. It's not what it used to be, but right now it's the only way I can imagine myself making a living. When I'm pulling up a chuckle from the gut, putting a smile on somebody's face, I feel like I'm doing something good, that I'm actually contributing, because the energy coming up on that corner is gonna carry past right on down the street. It's all about the shits and giggles.

Kenny the Silver Cowboy from Mississippi

I'm dying. Don't ask me what from. I don't know. It's just calling on me. I can feel it. I felt my mother's death. I felt my brother's death. Now I feel mine and it's the same feeling, I know it's there. I don't know when, but I know it's coming.

Growing up I never thought I'd be a real cowboy. I thought cowboy days was over with. I still saw every Jesse James movie they ever made, always had me a cowboy hat, pistols and rifles, you name it. Used to go hunting pigs down in Bufard Pussard County. Hunting pigs, you take a pistol and a rifle, 'cause them pigs are smart. They set a trap for you and chase you up a tree, you're gonna need that pistol to shoot your way down.

When I was eighteen years old, I came down to New Orleans with a cowboy hat. I always wore a cowboy hat, and cowboy hats were bad luck down here. You wore a cowboy hat, you went to jail. That's just the way it seemed to me, and I stopped wearing 'em. They ended up in jail. Then in '93, when I came out here as The Silver Cowboy, I said I'll just go to jail with this thing, but I'm keeping it. But the police seen me coming down the street, "Hey, how you doing?" They didn't bother me at all.

For the first five years I kept working at the labor hall, because it was a regular ticket, but for the last ten years, I been taking care of myself. Haven't had a real job since then. Don't spend any money on drinking, cause I don't drink. Haven't drank for years. I pay my rent and electric. It's slower on the streets now, but you can't get upset. If somebody comes by and takes a picture and don't throw nothing in the bucket, there's gonna be someone else that comes along that makes it up for you. God's gonna send somebody along to give me what I need. Since the accident I'm a real strong believer in God.

Last spring, I was walking across the street and got hit by a car. I was in that coma for eight weeks. I don't remember nothing of the accident. When the Lord brought me back from the dead, he told me, pass my word. I always knew the Lord, but I never preached his word to people. Now I tell this story nine, ten times a day to people.

Somewhere along the line before I die, and take my word for this and mark it, He's got something special in mind for me. If it's saving someone's life, I don't know. If it's doing something special in his name, then that's what it is. I don't know what it is yet. But it's something, and I know it's coming too. But as far as my life, it's not going very far. I'm through. But I'm prepared for it, because I know that the good Lord has a special spot for me up in heaven, not in hell. He's not gonna let the devil take me.

And when I get up there I'm gonna be a silver angel.

Maria from Boston

I grew up with the typical Catholic upbringing back when the nuns could still hit you if you didn't shut up and keep still. Maybe that's why I'm good at being a statue. At least now nobody smacks me with a ruler.

My mother, daughter of immigrants, told me that when I graduated high school I had to go to college or else I'd get kicked out of the house. Then when I started college, she said I better study something that would get me a job, because she wasn't going to support me when I was done — cut off from the family. I would have loved to have studied art or English. But no, I knew I needed a guaranteed job, so I became a nurse.

For ten years I worked as a nurse in Boston, New York and finally New Orleans. I hated every minute of it, the smell, the schedule. The worst was being around death all the time. It was horrible. In 1995 I decided that I'd had enough, so I quit and started tending bar.

There was this one fellow who worked as a statue out in Jackson Square who used to come in every night and change all of his coins into bills. When I saw how much money it was, I thought it sounded pretty good. I love to sew, so putting together the outfit was a lot of fun. Some people say I look like Ms. Havisham from *Great Expectations*, but I really wasn't trying to represent anyone in particular. I was just looking for something that would cover the most amount of skin so I'd need less makeup. This stuff isn't cheap.

Out here I do nothing. It's not that hard. Once in a while some drunk will try to do something lewd to get me upset, but I just keep quiet. Sometimes, I have to smack somebody with the flower pot, but that's pretty rare. Once, there was a guy who tried to light me on fire, but one of the Tarot card readers jumped on him and put it out. After the storm I had to quit for two years, because they're weren't as many tourists. I just started up a few weeks ago and things seem to be picking up. All and all, I'm pretty satisfied. Back when I was a nurse, I was running all over the place, and I never had a chance to really enjoy looking at the world. Now I just stand back and watch the crazy people through the glasses.

Maria

Valentino from Macedonia

In Yugoslavia it was nice childhood. We were real free, untouched by the system. Tito was one of the coolest dictators you ever see. Before the war there were no guns. We used to go with five or ten of us and make bonfires and play guitars on a hill where you can see the city down in the valley. It was good childhood, but to make a living, it is very hard to do anything honest and make it. I remember when I was seventeen, I was on the hill and I looked at the full moon and said, "God take me to America please."

When I was twenty and my hormones were kicking, I decided that I had to get out of my parents control, so I went hitchhiking playing music on the street in Europe. In France, I saw a man do marionette on the strings like a violin player. No one would stop to listen to me, playing the real music, but this man with the puppet had a big crowd.

When I got back home, I decided to make my own puppets. My dad he built all these shoes and constructions and everything. Black puppets, white puppets all smooth and cool. Me and my brother and my best friends went on tour with a five-piece puppet band. We played Louis Jordan, Joy Jackson, a lot of swing. The people loved us. Many people heard we did well and started doing it. Big movement came out of our country. We didn't talk, we just did the music. Everybody thought we were from the United States. When they found out we were Yugo, it would be like a total disappointment.

The Balkans never had a great reputation. They've always been poorer than the Western Europeans. They always feel like a higher class than you. In Germany when the police see your passport they say, "We don't like Yugo here. If we see you tomorrow, we will send you back to your country." In Holland I had people taking my marionette like a football for fun. We had the best response from the American tourists there. That was one of the reasons we wanted to come here.

To come to USA is hard, but I had a girlfriend who was doing the puppets with us who could get us to Canada. I remember the first time we played on the streets in Toronto, I was thinking these people are so nice compared to Amsterdam. It was like another planet. We did

some festivals, but then the others wanted to go back home.

Me and my girlfriend went on to New York. It was cold there, so someone told us we could work in Orlando, Florida. We hated it. We thought, man if this is America we're out of this country. We met a guy who said to put all of our stuff in a truck and come do our show at a bar in Pensacola. It was a Navy bar we were working in, nobody cared about puppets. The man said, I can give you a ride back to Orlando, or I can give you a ride to New Orleans. So we came here. We didn't have anything to lose.

New Orleans was immediately a winner. Everybody was so nice from the beginning. No one here cares that I'm Yugo, after I'd been here a year they say, hey man, you're from New Orleans. We made so many friends. We did so many parties together. In 1991 we did our first Jazz Fest. Sixteen years later, I'm still here and I still love performing for the people of New Orleans. Whatever you desire usually happens to you. Sometimes I can't even believe I'm here.

Jerik Danerson from New Orleans

"Oh dear gods, it's the sorcerer's apprentice, I can smell them coming every time."

In my young manhood in Hollywood, California, I was in a coffee shop, and I saw a man who reminded me of Merlin doing exactly what I do now. Those were his exact first words to me. He was a hard ass, but he taught me well. After a year of apprenticeship he said, "My curse on you is that you will become me. Someday someone will come up to you and the cycle will begin all over again." Sure enough, his prophecy came true. In the thirty-five years I've spent as a reader on Jackson Square, I've taught more than a few other people how to do this.

One of the biggest misconceptions about what I do is that people think I can tell the future. I'm not a fortuneteller. There's nothing paranormal about palmistry, it's a rote skill like reading a map. The hand is a microcosm of a human personality. When I read a hand, I'm just sharing the benefit of my forty-one years of education in palmistry. Believe it or not, I actually wrote a masters thesis on palmistry. I've even taught classes on palmistry at community colleges. Fortunately, I make more money in Jackson Square than I did teaching college. When you're a widower with six daughters to raise, you have to do what you can to make ends meet. I'm thankful that I've been able to accomplish that doing something I enjoy.

Mostly I'm an entertainer. That's what I have to offer for four out of five people who sit down in my chair. But for that fifth person who's looking for something deeper, I try to offer sound advice on the matter of living. Mostly it's about common sense. When someone asks me advice on something, I'm not pulling it out of the beyond, I'm pulling it out of my life. Say, you're having a problem with your daughter, having raised six daughters, I don't need a Tarot deck to give you advice about it.

I suppose I'm something like a psychologist. Carl Jung actually wrote three essays on the Tarot in which he said that the cards are nothing more than seventy-eight archetypes for the collective subconscious. When you shuffle the cards, your connection to the

collective subconscious is setting the pattern. All the reader does is interpret them. I don't feel that the cards are all knowing. What do you expect from seventy eight pieces of printed card stock? When somebody comes to me and says they think that their grandmother is trying to contact them from the dead, I tell them that my cell phone doesn't reach that far. You've come to the least mystical reader on Jackson Square.

Basically, I offer people a mirror of confirmation. Half the time the people already know the answers to their questions themselves. But here I am, a complete stranger, saying, yes, you should hold out for the college of your choice. Yes, you should pick that as your career path. I just give them a little inspiration to follow through on their decisions. Do you remember the story of Walt Disney's Dumbo? Now Dumbo could fly because he had large ears, but the only reason he believed it was because Timothy the Mouse gave him a magic feather. It never hurts to hand somebody a magic feather.

One of the most rewarding and challenging aspects of working out here in the Square is that I'm constantly talking with the street kids. Forty years ago, I was a street kid myself. I know what it's like to travel in a boxcar and hitchhike. A lot of these kids come from dysfunctional homes, so they really look to me to play that parental role. They call me Daddy Bear.

Heather*: Daddy Bear, You don't need some help out here?

Jerik: I've got all the help I need. This is not a high impact job.

Heather: I'm supposed to be working for Jazz Fest, temporary of course, but I want something permanent.

Jerik: What kind of job would you like?

Heather: CAD. Computer Assisted Design.

Jerik: You're probably not going to find that on Jackson Square.

Heather: I don't come here that much.

* alias

Jerik with his daughter and fellow reader Fox

Sidewalk Saints

Jerik: You're missing my point. If that's your dream, it's not going to be under the park bench over there, darling. If you go back to school and study computer assisted design, get a degree in it, that would be the ticket to your dream, honey. You're not going to find it in the squat. You're not going to find it on the park bench. You're not going to find it with people smoking catnip on the river. If you want to make change in your life, you have to be the active participant.

Heather: You think I could really go to college?

Jerik: That's not a difficult question, Heather. The answer is yes.

I'm glad you got to see my little intervention with Heather. That's why they call me the Godfather of Jackson Square, which is funny, because I never planned on being an old person. But honestly, over the past thirty-five years, as much as this place has changed, it's still basically the same place. We had street kids then. We have street kids now. We had drunk tourists then. We have drunk tourists now. It's still probably one of the best places in the world to go and interact with all types of human beings. I just hope they don't put a fence around it and start charging admission.

Editor's Note: Jerik Danerson passed away from complications due to acute pancreatitis on March 14, 2009 at University Hospital. He consciously refused life support before leaving this world. Rest in peace Jerik. You are missed.

Jerik entertains for a Haunted History tour group.

Regina Rhodes from St. Louis

I first came to live in New Orleans in 1975. My mother had a real bad case of the drunken meanies and it just got to the point where I figured I was safer on the street than I was in my own house. It was April and still pretty cold up in St. Louis. I didn't have much by way of clothes, so I figured I'd get where it was warmer. I was a very frightened, very hostile, angry-at-the-world teenager, and this city just took me in. People gave me food, a place to stay and got me a job waiting tables. It's been my home ever since.

I started reading palms in Jackson Square in 1984. I'd just left my old man and was working at a terrible bar on Decatur Street staying up all night dealing with drunks, which made it really hard to be at home taking care of my two kids. One night, I was coming home at the crack of dawn, and I ran into Jerik setting up his table. I asked him what he was doing and he told me he was reading palms. I said, oh, I can do that. You mean you can get paid for it? Duh. We got to talking and Jerik said he would show me the ropes.

Jerik really showed me showmanship and presentation — how to make a perfect stranger sit down and feel comfortable. I'll always be grateful for that. After working with Jerik for a few weeks, he decided I was ready to set up my own table. At first, I was terrified, but then I had a gentleman give me fifty dollars for a single reading. The Worlds Fair was here, so the city was full of tourists. Pretty soon I was able to quit my job and do this full time. It worked out well because I could be at home when my kids needed me.

Over the years I must have done thousands of readings. People might not always remember me, but I'd like to think that some of what I see in people's palms and in the cards opens up a door so that they look deeper into what's going on in their own lives. Sometimes it has a ripple effect. It's like when you drop a pebble in a bucket of water, the waves that hit the side are bigger than the original splash. That's what I love about being out here, seeing those waves rolling.

Regina Rhodes

Alobar from New York City

I got my first Tarot deck in 1967 when I was going to Cornell. It was mainly for my own exploration, but before long people were coming to me for advice even though I still had the instruction book in my hand. I never thought I'd make a dime off of it, but it was a great way to pick up women.

When I left college I started working at an antiwar print shop in Ithaca. It was long hours and low pay, but I figured at least I was helping change the world. When the war ended, the movement lost a lot of momentum and the shop moved out to California. I kind of had a shift of consciousness where I realized that the change the world needed was going to be on a personal level rather than a political level, so I bought myself a farm and started growing magic mushrooms. I did that for about ten years — made good money with it and helped a lot of people reprogram themselves.

Coming into the eighties you had Ronald Reagan with his War on Drugs. Every day, they had thousands of kilograms of cocaine coming in from Columbia, but of course they had to go after the hippies that weren't hurting anybody. Pretty soon we had surveillance planes flying over. When the cops started closing in, we had to shut down our operation. When a friend offered me a ride to New Orleans, I went.

I first started doing readings in the Square in 1992. At first it was difficult, because I'd hung out with so many countercultural people who understood paganism and magic that I wasn't sure that I could relate to ordinary people in the street. Pretty soon I realized that everybody asks the same kind of questions. It's about their girlfriend or boyfriend. It's about their job. It's about their health or whether their going to have kids. Over time, I've learned to be a little more direct with people with my answers.

A couple years ago I had I had one reading with a great big obese lady chain smoking cigarettes who asked me if her health is going to remain good. I looked at her and said, "You wouldn't know good health if it came by and bit you in the ass." She started getting tears in her eyes, and then I said that she was on a fast track to being a cripple

or dead. You've gotta change your lifestyle.

She gave me a good tip.

I can't always be completely honest. Last week I had a woman stop by, and she wanted to know what the future was going to be like for her grandchildren. Now, the way I see it, with global warming, the number of mammals on this planet is going to go down dramatically. The United States is going to go down the tubes and eventually the human race will be extinct. I just told her that things are uncertain, and that she should makes sure that she gives her grandkids good values, so that they can deal with whatever happens.

When I think about the future of New Orleans, I see the Blasted Tower — massive disruption. On the surface it's a negative card, but what it really means is letting go of the past and learning how to do things differently.

Jeremy Kerr Ph.D. from Lake Charles, Louisiana

Basically, I go out and find people who are having a good time, take their picture and print them a copy on the spot with my portable printer. Sometimes they give me tips. I don't like to hustle people. There's a lot of good hustlers in the Quarter, but I'm not one of them. I'm assertive, but I'm not aggressive. It's not that hard to get people's attention, because I've got all these flashing lights on my hat, and in case you didn't notice I wear a skirt.

Sometimes people react like I'm a freak. I am a freak, but it has nothing to do with the skirt. Men wore skirts for thousands of years. It's the oldest unisex garment in human history. When Adam and Eve left the Garden of Eden, what were they wearing? A skirt! When David fought Goliath, what was he wearing? A skirt! If there ever was a symbol of sexual equality, it's the skirt. It's not since the invention of the fucking sewing machine that men wore pants. I'm just a straight guy who likes wearing skirts. It's the ultimate garment. Plus, I've got nice legs, so why should girls have all the fucking fun?

I've definitely taken a lot of shit. Leading up to Mardi Gras, I almost got my ass kicked everyday. There's a lot of new people in town since Katrina, and they don't quite grasp that this town is all about freedom of expression. Just before Mardi Gras, I was ready to take every skirt in my closet, which I've got about forty, and just say the fuck with this, I'm giving it up, I'm done. But then Mardi Gras came along and you've got hundreds of half naked people walking down the street. It makes it crystal clear to the newcomers that this city is all about letting people be whatever they want to be.

I'm out here to document that spirit.

John Brown from Hollywood

My parents gave me my first telescope when I was twelve-years-old. I used to sit on the front lawn of our house in Hollywood and ask the people walking around looking for movie stars if they wanted a look at the real thing.

The only time in my life I didn't have a telescope was the three years I spent in Vietnam. I was a drafted, otherwise I wouldn't have gone. The last thing you wanted to do over there was look up. No thank you, not with bullets whizzing by my ear. I was damn glad to get out of there, but when I came back, everything that I had was gone, my girlfriend, my job, my apartment. I haven't had a regular job since then. If it weren't for my parents, I don't know what I would have done.

After I got discharged, I had five hundred dollars saved up, but instead of buying a car like most guys, I bought an old eight inch F7 telescope. I set it up in my parents' yard and looked at the sky. Mentally, I was out there somewhere. I imagined what a quasar would look like or what it would be like to go through the center of a black hole. They say that black holes are just like a hurricane, if you go through the exact center nothing would happen to you, but if you entered through the walls you'd be devastated.

My dad was the jazz musician Pud Brown. He was the first white guy to play with Louis Armstrong. They were good friends. Back in the thirties my dad used to hide Louis in his house in Shreveport when he was running from the mob. I remember meeting him when I was six-years-old, and he said in his deep voice what a cute kid I was. My dad was always really proud of me. It didn't matter that I didn't become a musician. In 1974 my family moved down here so my dad could play regular gigs in the Quarter. I went with them.

I started setting up my scope in front of Café DuMonde. At that time the Moonwalk was a train yard four tracks deep. The benches used to be filled with hobos riding in on the freights. Back then, people used to line up on the sidewalk to look through the scope.

I've turned a lot of people on to astronomy that otherwise would never have discovered it. A few years ago I had an astronomy professor come by and tell me that my telescope was what got him

started. Then on the other hand there's the people who don't think that my telescope is real. They think I've got slides hidden inside the eyepiece and they get angry at me and call me a liar. At first it hurt me a little, but now I'm used to it. I suppose that's how Galileo must have felt.

Once in a while, Christians come by and their kids want to know if they can see God. I show them the constellation Signus the Savior. It's always directly over your head on Easter morning. One time, I was explaining the meanings of the stars for the early Christians to the this elderly lady, and she thought it was so beautiful that she broke down in tears.

Probably the best experience I've had out here was when a couple stopped by with a son who was autistic. He looked completely blank, but once he saw the moon and all the craters and mountains, it just sparked something in his brain and he got all excited. His parents were amazed because nothing had affected him like that before.

Overall, I feel that the city appreciates what I'm doing. Around 1980 the city counsel started passing laws regulating the street vendors in the Quarter. The counsel members took a vote on who should stay and who should go. The artists got some votes. The fortune tellers didn't get any votes at all. I got the most number of votes.

Up till Katrina, I was doing alright. I was staying in my dad's old apartment, but the roof got destroyed so I had to move. I used to pay $425, but now I pay almost $800 for one room. It's getting harder to make rent.

I just turned sixty, so I can't always work as hard as I used to. I have to take it easy sometimes. About four years ago I started having seizures for some reason, and I wound up in the hospital in a coma because I hit my head real hard. While I was in the VA, they told me that I had PTSD and symptoms of exposure to Agent Orange. I had no idea. Since then I've been trying to get disability. For four years I've been kind of battling with the Veterans Administration. You have to jump through all the hoops. It's like a nightmare.

I'm an astronomer not an astrologer, so I can't tell you exactly what I see in my future. Hopefully I'll be out here doing this 'til I'm ninety. If I won the lottery, I'd still do this. I'd probably just buy a better telescope.

Warpo

Bobby Maverick

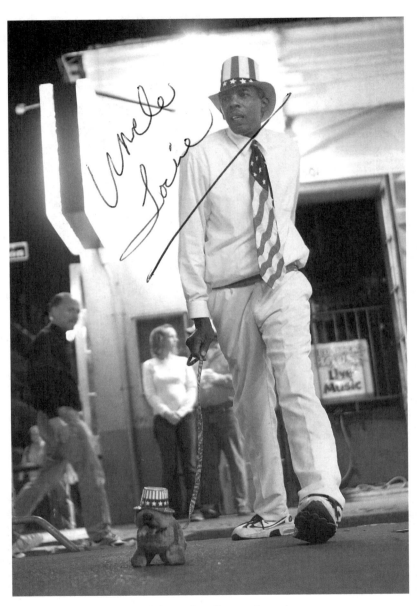

Uncle Louie

Lil Countrie

Dragon Master Showcase

C-Los

Dragon Master Showcase

Miss Pearl

Fox

February, 2008

Marzipan

Cajun

Robotron

Noel Freeman and Glenn Preston
Da Truth Brass Band

Travis Carter
Da Truth Brass Band

Tyrus Chapman

Darren Towns and Antoine Coleman
To Be Continued Brass Band

Daven Vance
To Be Continued Brass Band

Chris Davis
To Be Continued Brass Band

Sean Roberts
To Be Continued Brass Band

Bernard Adams
To Be Continued Brass Band

Darryl Parlow
To Be Continued Brass Band

Next Generation Brass Band

Flo

Eve Kuffner
Debauche
177

Jesse Stoltzfus
Debauche
178

Eli Pritykin

Debauche

179

Jesse

Corey
The Music Box

Jeff
The Music Box

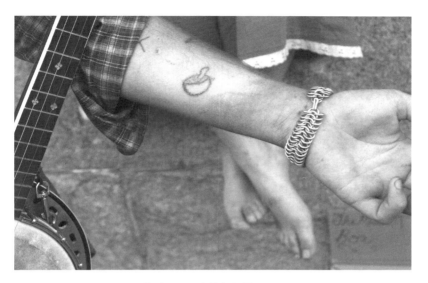

Poke and Stick Tattoo

Beer Elfing

The Hail Seizures
Visiting From Olympia
184

Scottie and Kaylee

Dwight

Blind Boy Troy
"The Pope"

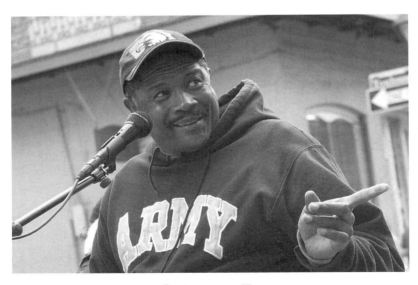

Stoney B.

Jay-Ray & Gee

Zack and Walker

Ross Harmon

Doreen Ketchens
"Queen Clarinet"

Reverend Coydog

also available from Jim Flynn and Curbside Press

Stranger to the System

life portraits of a New York City
homeless community

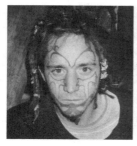  

10/13/08 burning the midnight oil at the Steven Spring Foundation warehouse

About the Editor

Jim Flynn was born in Albany, New York in 1977. For nine years he taught special education in Manhattan public high schools. He began interviewing New Orleans street performers during a week vacation in February, 2008 and moved here permanently in September. The crunch to have this book available for the performers to sell on the street during Jazz Fest did not leave him with sufficient time to write a quality introduction. Visit sidewalksaints.com to read about his personal experiences with the project. Any editorial or design suggestions for the second edition would be greatly appreciated.